3244332 MITCHELL

Splendid Sisters

SPLENDID SISTERS

A story of the
planning, construction, and operation
of the Shaw Savill liners

SOUTHERN CROSS & NORTHERN STAR

by ALAN MITCHELL

GEORGE G. HARRAP & CO. LTD
London · Toronto · Wellington · Sydney

To
PEGGY AND JOHN

First published in Great Britain 1966
by GEORGE G. HARRAP & CO. LTD
182 High Holborn, London, W.C.1

Composed in Monotype Imprint and printed by
Morrison & Gibb Ltd, London and Edinburgh
Made in Great Britain

Preface

THIS is the first book of its type that I have attempted—part story, part documentary, and not an easy razor edge on which to balance. My main objective has been to try to make it readable . . . to revive pleasant memories for those who have been associated with or sailed in *Southern Cross* and *Northern Star*, and to interest those who are yet to travel in these fine ships. I thank the many people who helped me with information, and in particular John MacConochie for the encouragement he has always given me.

ALAN MITCHELL

WESTHUMBLE,
DORKING, SURREY
December 1964

Contents

Illustrations

CHAPTER ONE

Engines Aft

SHE would be the first of her type in the world—a 20,000-ton liner, carrying over a thousand passengers, but no cargo, a one-class tourist ship. Her engines would be aft instead of midships, and she would drive round the world in seventy-six days, four times a year, on a strict time-schedule, arriving at and leaving ports punctually. She would be something really new in shipping.

Basil Sanderson, chairman and managing director of the Shaw Savill Line, stirred in his bed.

It was just after two o'clock, the dawn of a July morning some two or three hours away. The sky was clear and starlit. The tall trees surrounding Ayot Bury were dark shadows, the garden a pool of black. It was a quiet, tranquil place, and what was now the barn had been built in the fifteenth century by a Hertfordshire farmer as his homestead.

Through years of habit Sanderson's light had been out at ten o'clock, and now, after four hours' sleep, he had awakened with his mind rested, refreshed, and alert. It was a time, he found, when problems seemed to settle into perspective. Not that there should be many of them today—Wednesday, July 16th, 1952. They had been resolved, for the time being anyway.

Engines aft—not midships. That had been his main problem over the new ship . . . how to persuade fellow directors, naval architects, superintendents, to support and agree with his belief that if there were no cargo-holds in a ship the engine-room could be moved to the extreme end.

It would mean that something like three-quarters of her space would be free from the clutter of uptakes around the engine and the funnel, of skylights and casings. This space would be used for the comfort and convenience of passengers, particularly in the lay-out of the lounges. There would also be wide areas of deck for sports and promenades. Everybody would be able to roam freely, with no sense of restriction or division of classes.

It seemed a logical belief, especially as tankers and aircraft-carriers had their engines aft. Yet there had been opposition from naval architects and technicians.

"Dangerous . . . impossible . . . trimming and stability would be too big a problem . . . asking for trouble."

His technical staff at the Royal Albert Dock—experts on ship design and construction—had not gone along with him, confirming their doubts after conversations with others in the industry.

Yet Sanderson was sure that he was right.

All his life he had been interested in ships and their design, from the time when he had grown up in a family background of shipping in Liverpool. He had seen many changes since then, but many old and stereotyped ideas persisted. For instance, as he had recently told the Institution of Naval Architects, there had been no real advance in the design of cargo-ships since the days of the Phoenicians. Now, as then, cargo was still brought alongside a hatch, lifted thirty feet or more into the air, swung a like distance, then lowered another thirty feet or so into position.

"A less inspiring and more wasteful exercise in ballistics it would be difficult to devise," he had remarked.

He appreciated the structural difficulties in designing a hull of the strength and type to permit a measure of horizontal loading as opposed to vertical. But he had also asked whether there could not be new ideas leading to economy of effort. Coupled with revolution in design might come the elimination of such anachronisms as masts and the projecting vertical funnel.

Whatever changes there might be in the future design of cargo-ships, he was convinced that new ideas such as engines aft should be adopted for ships carrying passengers only. Undoubtedly there would be questions of trim, for the stern would tend to be heavy with the weight of the engines transferred, but there were ways of overcoming this.

His arguments and beliefs had not been accepted, however, and he had not persisted.

There had been agreement that the Shaw Savill Line should build a ship to carry passengers, but no cargo. This was sound policy because, with delays in loading, cargo-passenger vessels were not only uneconomic, but infuriating to passengers, who never could be sure when they might sail or arrive. But engines aft—no.

So the new ship had been put out to tender, and this had been won by Harland and Wolff, the Belfast builders with whom Shaw Savill had a long association. The point whether there should be a change in the position of the engines was not mentioned.

Then, at virtually the last moment, David Swan, the senior assistant superintendent engineer, a Scot in his sixty-second year, who had been with the Line since 1919 and was soon to retire, walked into his room.

Sanderson had always liked Swan, who had an air of rugged, Scottish individualism, and who leavened bluntness with dry wit. The sea and engines were in his blood. While still a small boy his grandfather had told him stories of days in the Royal Navy breaking up the opium trade on the China coast. When he grew older Swan decided to combine engines with the sea, and after his schooling at Rutherford College, Newcastle, he served an apprenticeship with Clarke, Chapman as a marine engineer, and then entered the Wallsend Slipway and Engineering Company as a draughtsman on naval construction. In 1919 he joined Shaw Savill as a junior engineer until coming ashore in 1925 with his first-class certificate and settling in the office of the superintendent engineer in the Royal Albert Dock.

Swan had taken no part in the discussions on the position of the engines in the new ship, but he was well aware of the differences of opinion—and he agreed with Sanderson, for he himself had been arguing for engines to be placed aft in cargo-ships. This idea had been rejected on the ground that it would be impossible to maintain trim in port while cargo was being loaded and unloaded. But Swan could see no good reason why a passenger-ship must have her engines midships, or why her funnel should not unload its smoke and fumes at the stern instead of smudging the ship from her middle. As for trim, he knew this could be kept constant by the distribution of distilled water as ballast.

Swan had come in and spoken with his usual bluntness, and Sanderson remembered how amused and gratified he had been to hear his own theories expounded.

It had been the turning-point. From their talk there developed conversations in Belfast with the builders' directors and the Line's marine and engineer superintendents. Rupert Cameron, the builders' assistant naval architect, said that if the ship was to have no cargo-holds there was no reason why she should not have her engines aft. Norman Miller, the Line's assistant naval architect, produced plans, and discussions in Belfast continued. Designs for the new type of passenger liner were completed and costs reassessed. Harland and Wolff said they were ready to confirm the changes at a formal meeting—today.

Sanderson drifted into sleep for another hour or two.

He was up and dressed at half-past five and in his study, reading papers, brooding over aspects of his wide range of directorships . . . the Bank of England, Furness Withy, the Ford Motor Company, Dalgety and New Zealand Loan, the British Maritime Trust, the Finance Corporation for Industry. He worked for two hours, after breakfast caught his usual train from Welwyn Garden City to Broad Street, and relaxed in his corner seat with *The Times* crossword puzzle.

The morning was fine and summery as he strode from Broad Street to the narrow canyon of Leadenhall Street, with its greyish buildings, and went up to his room in the Shaw Savill offices on the first floor of Cunard House—number 88. It was a modest room, subdued, with a large desk, partly panelled in mahogany, with a matching light-brown carpet. Two models of sailing-ships in glass cases caught the eye— the Line's famous clipper, the 1058-ton *Crusader*, built in 1869, and the grain-carrier *Passat*, sister to the *Pamir*.

As the time for the meeting approached he went over the main points with Errington Keville, his deputy chairman and general manager, and greeted Captain A. E. Lockhart and Robert Craig, the marine and engineer superintendents, and others. He had a smile for Swan.

They all welcomed the men from Harland and Wolff —John Baillie and Strachan, both directors, Pounder, the engineer designer, and Cameron; and then sat round a long, green baize-covered table in the corner of Sanderson's room.

That evening, when the train took him back to Welwyn Garden City and he had completed his crossword puzzle, Sanderson recalled the main points . . . the personal message of support Baillie had brought from Sir Frederick Rebbeck, chairman and managing director of Harland and Wolff . . . the technicalities.

The new design with engines aft meant there would be twenty extra cabins to take forty-four more passengers, and deck space would be increased by 17 per cent—two immediate gains.

There would be some extra cost . . . about £156,000. This included the extension of the beam by one foot to seventy-seven feet, but there would be some saving on furnishing and decorating . . . about £24,000. The builders' revised, final estimate was just over £3,546,000, compared with the original £3,390,000 . . . not too bad when set against the additional earnings and convenience for passengers. (The final capital cost agreed with the Inland Revenue was £4,565,255, of which the builders accounted for £3,846,818.)

There had been other points . . . the idea of using laminated plastic linings instead of plywood to cover bulkheads and passages. Plywood needed to be painted regularly, but you couldn't waste time painting if the ship was to have a quick turn-round and maintain her schedule. Plastic could be washed or sponged. They'd have to look at the cost of plastic, however, which was uppish in price and limited in range.

There had been talk about power and speed . . . a margin of eighteen and a half to twenty and a quarter knots, giving a reserve if the ship were delayed by bad weather . . . mention of tank tests to check speeds . . . of wind-tunnel smoke tests at Teddington to select a funnel to keep fumes and smuts clear of the decks . . . of colours . . . of floodlighting. . . .

Delivery would be to schedule, despite the change in design—between December 1954 and January 1955. As for the question of trim and stability, an initial estimate was for a distilling plant to produce up to three hundred tons of fresh water a day, which should be enough to meet the needs of passengers and fill the ballast-tanks. . . .

Sanderson thought it had been a satisfying meeting . . . after all the earlier doubts. There would be complications as building proceeded, but that was normal.

The main point was that the new ship would be the first of her type: her engines would be aft, and not midships.

2

Steps to the Chair

IN July 1952 Basil Sanderson was fifty-eight, and the vigour of his intellect and his knowledge of shipping were valued by the Shaw Savill Line and in the City of London. Yet there had been a time when his entry into the shipping world had been opposed—by his father, Harold Sanderson, chairman of the Oceanic Steam Navigation Company (the White Star Line) and of several other companies, including Shaw Savill and the Aberdeen Line.

The Sandersons were a North Country family, and in the 1880's Harold accompanied his father, Richard, to New York, where they established the firm of Sanderson and Son. There Basil was born on June 19th, 1894, a second son. The same year Harold Sanderson joined Ismay, Imrie and Company, managers of the White Star Line, became a partner in 1899, and settled in Liverpool to manage the Line's interest there. In 1902 White Star was bought by the International Mercantile Marine Company, the American shipping combine. Harold Sanderson followed Bruce Ismay as president of IMMC in 1913. Subsequently, he was succeeded by P. A. S. Franklin, and became chairman in Europe of several of its companies.

In Liverpool, Basil Sanderson grew up in an atmosphere of ships and shipping, absorbing it as easily as he took to sport. At his public school, Rugby, he became as tall as his father (six foot one), excelled at swimming, boxing, and Rugby football, and was capped for all three. His height was an advantage in the second row of the scrum in school games, and when he toured with the Oxford side in Ireland in 1913–14; it also gave him a useful reach when he represented Rugby as a middleweight in the public-schools boxing competitions at Aldershot in 1911.

Sanderson did not win his match, but his keenness impressed a friend of his father's, Oscar Thompson of George Thompson and Company, managers of the Aberdeen Line, who invited him to London. There Oscar Thompson demonstrated the finer points of squash racquets, and took the rather reserved and shy boy, whose blue eyes lit with humour in his long, lean, narrow face when he smiled, to the old National Sporting Club. It was the night when a young French-man, Georges Carpentier, knocked out Bombardier Billy Wells in seventy seconds, a night Sanderson never forgot. Nor did he forget Oscar Thompson, from whom he was not to hear again for nearly ten years.

They were eventful years. Sanderson was eighteen when he left Rugby in 1912, and went up to Trinity College, Oxford, to read French literature.

He went with a warning from his father: when he came down he was to look for a career outside shipping.

"There is an overload of Sandersons in this industry," his father said—Harold Sanderson himself, his two brothers and three nephews, and Basil's elder brother, Winchester. He suggested law as an alternative.

If Sanderson had other ideas he did not disclose them, but applied himself to Oxford, where his studies did not interfere with his boxing and Rugby football. On the night of October 13th, 1913, he won both cruiser and heavyweight Oxford titles on points, and in 1912 and 1913 he was noticed in the Trinity pack.

In December 1913 and in the spring of 1914 he was picked occasionally for the Oxford team, and turned out for Richmond. The odds were that he would be awarded his blue and play against Cambridge in the autumn.

But when December arrived he was a lieutenant in the Duke of Lancaster's Own Yeomanry. He had given up his third year at Trinity and the prospect of a degree, and put on his uniform in September, a few weeks after Sir Edward Grey had observed that the lamps were going out all over Europe. By June 1915 he was in action in France.

He survived the following years of slaughter, and lived with distinction. He was seconded to become Divisional machine-gun officer to the 23rd Infantry Division, and awarded the Military Cross in 1916, on the Somme. Promoted Brigade Major to the 126th Brigade, he was mentioned twice in dispatches and, during the final German advance in 1918, pinned on a bar to his M.C. He was subsequently promoted to G.S.O.2 of the 41st Infantry Division, and was recommended for the Distinguished Service Order, and his Divisional Commander was incensed when a Brevet Majority was gazetted instead. The Belgians gave him their Croix de Guerre.

After the War Sanderson, as G.S.O.2 to the 41st Infantry Division with the British Army of Occupation, was in charge of demobilization. Civilian jobs were scarce in 1919, and nobody was being demobilized without a post to go to. Now twenty-five, he had no inclination to return to Oxford or to remain in the Army. To hasten his release, he suggested that his father might find a position for him in the shipping industry; but while the War had changed many things it had not altered Harold Sanderson's opinion about the "over-load". Nevertheless he was willing that Basil should join the White Star Line in Liverpool—but on one condition: after two years he would find work in business other than shipping.

Sanderson was happy enough in Liverpool, but realized he would have to find other employment by the middle of 1921. Nobody, it seemed, wanted a former major, whatever his War record or his public-school and university background. There was one opening—on the Stock Exchange—but this had no appeal.

Doubtful about his future, he went to Switzerland for a ski-ing holiday over Christmas 1920. Fortune seemed against him still, for he found himself not on the ski slopes, but in hospital with scarlet fever. Life, which had been so full of promise at school and university, and then a matter of luck in France, was now a series of setbacks.

It was at this moment that a letter arrived from London. The writing was unfamiliar, and he glanced at the signature—Oscar Thompson. The intervening years rolled away, and he was back at the ringside watching Carpentier and Wells. He was touched that Thompson should remember him, and, idly, he began to read.

Moments later all his depression and introspection had melted like snow under a hot sun. Oscar Thompson was offering him a post with his Company—the Aberdeen Line—and with his father's approval.

It was reluctant approval nevertheless. It had taken all the persuasive powers of both Thompson and of Franklin in New York to overcome his father's dislike of anything suggesting nepotism.

There was no doubt of Sanderson's reply, and in March 1921, a few months short of his twenty-seventh birthday, he started in the Thompson office in Billiter Square, a rather strange world where he had no official title or position.

Oscar welcomed him and took him into a small room in which there were two large table desks, one counterposed to the other, with four chairs. Oscar occupied one, two more were filled by Duff Henderson and Raymond Jones, and the fourth was for him. It took him a little time to settle down, for everybody talked freely about his work, and at first it was difficult to shut out the conversation and concentrate on his own work.

But he observed many things. First that Oscar had a brilliant mind, but was bored by detail. He would provide an answer to a problem, leaving others to put it into effect. His knowledge of the shipping industry was massive, ranging from design—his father Cornelius had designed the famous clipper *Thermopylae*—to finance. His interests were wide, and he explained Einstein's theory of relativity with fluent ease. His methods of introducing Sanderson into the business were unorthodox, for he would send his protégé to a conference as the Aberdeen Line's representative with the sole instruction: "You do what you think is right."

It was rather like being thrown into the deep end and told to swim, but it sharpened the mind. Sanderson learned many things rapidly, among them that the Aberdeen Line's five cargo-passenger ships were not showing a profit, and that at some convenient stage it was to merge with Shaw Savill.

Once he was familiar with the London office he was sent to Australia, where he spent over a year in the various ports, and also up-country, and then he went on to New Zealand for four months. When he returned to Billiter Square he had a firm grasp of the affairs of both the Aberdeen and Shaw Savill Lines in those countries. He was appointed manager when Henderson retired.

In 1927 the long-mooted merger took place. A

Scotsman, John Macmillan, general manager of Shaw
Savill, now directed the business of both Lines, with
Sanderson as manager. After six years he was a rising
figure in the shipping world, with a flair for dealing
with its intricacies, an appetite for work, and an
imaginative mind masked by his shy reserve, which,
to those who did not know him, sometimes made him
appear rather diffident and abrupt. Beneath it was a
warm friendliness; he was invariably referred to as
"Basil" or "B.S."

It was an eventful year for Sanderson domestically,
too, for he married Evelyn Ismay, the daughter of
Bruce Ismay, former chairman of the White Star
Line, and, after four years in London itself, went to
live at Highgate. In 1929 a daughter, Pauline Maud,
was born, and in 1931 he became the father of twins,
Alan Lindsay and Murray Lee.

Harold Sanderson's health was failing, and he
began to spend the winters in Rapallo, in Italy. He
died there in February 1932, at the age of seventy-one.
Whether or not his father was proud of his progress
in the shipping world after that initial opposition
Basil never knew. They were great friends, but the
family shyness closed certain doors.

Throughout the difficult and momentous years from
1927 to 1939 Sanderson's reputation continued to
grow. Many sought his opinions and advice. He became
president of the International Shipping Federation and
of the British Employers' Confederation, and chairman
of several organizations—among them the Shipping
Federation, the London General Shipowners' Society,
the National Council of Port Labour Employers. He
was also a member of the Council of the Chamber of
Shipping.

Away from his work, he was deeply content. He was
happily married; the children were growing up. In

1937 he and Evelyn decided to move from Highgate, and they chose Ayot Bury, deep in the peaceful quietness of Hertfordshire, which had its roots in Anglo-Saxon history. Farmed for centuries, the countryside had been little disturbed since the days of the Danish invasions, one of which ended in a massacre and a communal grave still recorded by the name Danesbury. The mansion of Ayot Bury dated from 1682, and was unchanged except for the addition of two wings; its adjacent farmhouse, dating from the fifteenth century, with its beamed and curving roof and ancient tiles, gave an atmosphere of character and mellowness. One room on the ground floor of the house was now converted into a schoolroom, and when various modernizations were completed the Sandersons moved in in the spring of 1938. Tennis courts were laid down, and a croquet lawn. There were horses in the stables.

Away from this rural calm, the outside world was noisy with the rumble of approaching war. After Munich, when Neville Chamberlain returned from his meeting with Hitler at Bad Godesberg, waving a useless piece of paper and forecasting "peace in our time", Sanderson, at the Government's invitation, agreed to form a Shipping in Ports Division in the event of war. His responsibility would be to oversee the movement of merchant ships in and out of ports in Britain and overseas.

In September 1939 he left Shaw Savill and Leadenhall Street and went to the Board of Trade offices in Whitehall. Six years were to pass before his company saw him again. He formed a team of men of wide experience and authority in the merchant shipping world, and when his Division was merged with the Ministry of Shipping they moved to Berkeley Square. In 1941 he was directing the combined Divisions of the

Ministry of Shipping and the Ministry of Transport. These were amalgamated and formed the Port and Transit Control of the Ministry of War Transport, supervising the cargo operations of merchant ships in all countries of the Western Allies, as well as controlling the ports in the United Kingdom—a gigantic task.

Sanderson welcomed it, for it helped him from grieving, though not from remembering. In the year after the War broke out Evelyn died, after being rolled on by a rearing horse. One of her close friends, whom they had both known for years, Mrs Elaine Ainley, widow of Henry Ainley, the actor, took over at Ayot Bury as châtelaine, caring for Pauline and the twins, and running the household. Work was now an anodyne for Sanderson. He commuted as regularly as possible to be with his children, but Ayot Bury could never be the same for him.

It was, indeed, lucky to be standing, for after the Battle of Britain some pilots—Germans, or possibly Italians—decided that the blitz of London was unhealthy and jettisoned in all forty-three bombs within four hundred yards of the house, and then circled to make up their mileage before returning to occupied Europe and reporting another successful mission. A stick of eleven bombs actually straddled Ayot Bury, one wrecking the tennis court a few yards from the house.

Occasionally, as the war at sea mounted and the toll of merchant ships grew, Sanderson was summoned to 10 Downing Street for meetings presided over by Winston Churchill. When at last his work at Berkeley Square was ended there was no doubt this time where his future lay.

In June 1945, a few weeks after VE Day, he ceased being a temporary civil servant, but he did not return immediately to Leadenhall Street. He was accustomed to exercise and keeping physically fit, and the years at the Ministry had left him no time for relaxation. Now he grumbled to himself when he wheezed at the top of a flight of stairs; for a man of fifty-one this was a poor show; he felt he was in no condition to direct the affairs of Shaw Savill immediately. These had been carried on since 1939 by John Macmillan, Errington Keville, Raymond Jones, and George Thompson. Macmillan retired at the end of April 1945, when victory in Europe was within sight.

Sanderson was to succeed Macmillan as managing director as soon as he was available. He was completely out of touch with the company's position, its finances, the effect of its War losses, and the extent of the trading it had been doing under requisition. He knew little or nothing of staff developments and promotions. He was certain of one thing: until he had thrown off the strain and fatigue of the War years and tuned himself up mentally and physically he could not face up to tackling the company's post-War problems.

Throughout the remainder of June and all July he stayed at Ayot Bury; Pauline and the twins were now in their teens. He played tennis, and worked in the gardens, setting out new rose and rhododendron beds, weeding and planting the kitchen garden, making hay, pulling down old buildings, shaping Ayot Bury just as he wanted it. When his muscles began to harden and he had lost his indoor pallor he began to visit Leadenhall Street once a week to get a gradual feel of the reins, but he kept to his eight weeks' break until, on August 1st, 1945, he returned as managing director.

He needed to be fit. The outlook for Shaw Savill was serious. Half its fleet was at the bottom of the ocean, and all but one of its cargo-ships built since 1930 had gone down. Its passenger-ships were now between twenty and thirty-four years old, the single exception being *Dominion Monarch*, launched in 1938, and still requisitioned for trooping. Only two cargo-ships, built and bought during the War, were modern.

Summed up, Shaw Savill had a greatly reduced elderly fleet which would have to be renewed and expanded. The cargo-ships could be kept going with some early renovation; but the passenger-ships, which also carried cargo, all needed reconditioning. A few were still working for the Ministry of Transport, and could be expected to be shabby and knocked about when they were no longer requisitioned. Although there would be some Government financial compensation, the company would face enormous bills.

It was a gigantic muddle. The main problem was: how to keep cargoes moving between Britain and Australia and New Zealand and to provide transport for passengers at the same time.

The long-term policy should be to build new ships, but should they be cargo or cargo-passenger? A building programme would be costly, and the £4 million due from the Government as compensation for War losses would be a drop in the ocean, for the price of ships had soared since 1939. The only immediate possible source of income was from an elderly, dilapidated fleet.

Sanderson decided to visit the customers, Australia and New Zealand, with whom there had been no close contact during the War years, and to assess their likely trends of trade, as well as the possibility of travel, before fixing on a firm policy. The important thing was to find out what the customers required.

On Friday, November 13th, three and a half months after returning to Leadenhall Street and on a date not as propitious as he could have wished, he was airborne in a bomber of RAF Transport Command bound for Sydney. It was March before he returned to London, and in the intervening period he went to all the company's offices in Australia and New Zealand and talked with every agent. He also had conversations with every State Premier in Australia, and in Wellington he saw Walter Nash, Minister of Finance, in the absence of Peter Fraser, the Prime Minister, who was overseas.

He learned that the War had not changed fundamentals. Britain would continue to be the main market for the primary produce of both countries for the foreseeable future; and if Britain needed food urgently for her still-rationed people, Australia and New Zealand were in equal need of industrial goods. Servicemen had to be brought home, and a post-War wave of immigration was anticipated. Empire sentiment was much the same, and once things settled down Australians and New Zealanders would be wanting to travel overseas. New markets would also be sought.

With this fresh background Sanderson proposed that the priorities for rebuilding the Shaw Savill fleet should be: new cargo-ships; the renovation of cargo-passenger ships; new cargo-passenger ships.

But there was an immediate demand for passenger berths and a long waiting-list. Shaw Savill had already ordered two new cargo-ships before he had left the Ministry. Because of the need for berths Sanderson cabled Leadenhall Street recommending two further ships with berths for eighty first-class passengers.

And there was still time to add berths to the two ships being built. All were to be in service by 1948—*Corinthic, Athenic, Ceramic,* and *Gothic.*

The value of his visit to Australia and New Zealand was to be proved during the next decade. By 1957 no fewer than twenty-three new ships were built for Shaw Savill at a cost of £27,500,000, and the number of pre-War ships was reduced to seven. The War compensation kitty of £4 million had been well managed and expended.

In 1947, a little more than a quarter of a century after he had read Oscar Thompson's letter in the Swiss hospital, Sanderson became chairman of Shaw Savill, and so succeeded his father.

Events in Australia and New Zealand influenced a basic change in Shaw Savill's policy for cargo-passenger ships during the next few years. Dock strikes, a shortage of labour, and other uncertainties meant a slower turn-round. Ships were delayed in ports for weeks and sometimes months. No passengers could be told with any certainty the date of their sailing.

Meanwhile crews had to be paid, costs rocketed, and at Leadenhall Street there were long discussions.

If an efficient and attractive passenger service were to be continued, then passenger-carrying would have to be divorced from cargo. But if there were a waiting-list of passengers now, what would be the position in five or ten years' time? What would be the effect of air travel on sea travel? What would be the most profitable, or, if not profitable, the most economic, route? How many passengers should be carried?

The questions were asked in Leadenhall Street and in the offices of the Line in New Zealand and Australia and South Africa. The marine, the engineering, the victualling superintendents were all consulted.

It was obvious that there would be no lack of passengers over the years ahead—particularly emi-grants to New Zealand and Australia. As for air-sea competition, they reasoned, each had its own function and attraction—the air for those who needed to travel long distances in a hurry; the sea for those to whom time was not all-important and to whom a ship offered a leisurely, comfortable holiday, and an opportunity of seeing one or more countries and several ports. There was room for both, and likely to be for as long ahead as could be seen.

The route should be round-the-world, instead of out to New Zealand via the Cape and back the same way. From Auckland it should be back to Southampton by way of Fiji and Tahiti and the Panama Canal, and any other ports that might be conveniently and profitably visited.

Experience with the migrant ship *New Australia* had proved that twelve hundred passengers could be catered for economically, and, as an insurance against a dwindling of travellers, a small number of the berths should be earmarked for settlers.

Sanderson and his directors finally made their momentous decision. They would build a 20,000-ton ship to carry some twelve hundred passengers and to run to a strict time-schedule. She would have a cruising speed of eighteen and a half knots and a reserve of over two knots to allow her to make up time for delays through weather or other causes. She would be entirely modern, and air-conditioning would be introduced. She would carry no cargo.

It was at this point that Sanderson had begun the debate on the engines being placed aft.

CHAPTER THREE

Change and Progress

ON that July evening in 1952, after the meeting
with Harland and Wolff, Sanderson set out on
a post-prandial stroll round his rose-bushes
at Ayot Bury. Although agreement on the new ship
having engines aft had been reached beforehand, and
the meeting was a formality in some respects, it had
been a day of quiet satisfaction. Shaw Savill was
going to do something new, something different, with
a big passenger liner. She would represent change
and progress as well as initiative and enterprise.
Would she be popular? Would she pay? Time would
tell.

Change and progress . . . initiative and enterprise.
They were synonymous with shipping. Oars to sail,
sail to steam . . . wood to coal, coal to oil . . . wooden
to iron to steel hulls . . . clipper and barque rigs to
cruiser sterns . . . from tiny wooden craft with a
handful of crew and passengers to huge liners providing
a service rivalling a hotel and with all the equipment—
and human problems—to be found in a village.

Every change was a reflection of thought and decision
and, in some cases, imagination. The men who directed
the affairs of the company down the years, including
his father, had contributed their fair share for nearly
a hundred years. A hundred years . . . back to the days
of sail . . . and Shaw and Savill who had first competed
with and then amalgamated with Patrick Henderson.

Sanderson wondered what they might think of the new ship when, in due course, she would sail on her maiden voyage with her funnel located over her stern.

Robert Shaw was a Scot, and he must have been quite a boy. He had thrown up his job at the age of thirty-five to launch out on his own in the New Zealand trade, a doubtful proposition in 1858. But he had obviously known all there was to know about it, for he had been in the freight department of Willis, Gann and Co., a London company which had been sending ships to the distant Colony for twenty years.

Perhaps Robbie Shaw had been restive at some lack of enterprise by his employers, perhaps his Scottish temper and ambition had irked them, and they wanted him out of the way. Whatever the reason, they had docked his salary—so the story went—and Shaw had stalked out after this affront to his pride and pocket. There might even have been more to it than that, for Walter Savill, a Londoner and then only twenty-one, had walked out as well; and the pair of them had been joined by others from Willis, Gann and Co. and set up in business on their own account. Perhaps they had worked it all out in advance in a coffee-house or over a pot of ale, or maybe a wee dram. They had no capital, but they had 'know-how'—the brokering and chartering of ships. They were soon in business as Shaw Savill and Co.

Their first advertisement appeared on the front page of *The Times* on Monday, March 15th, 1858. It began "New Zealand Goldfields", and in something over an inch of space said that the beautiful full-poop, river-built clipper *Chieftain*, A1, twelve years, 500 tons burthen, would sail from London docks "about 15th April" for Nelson direct. So she did, and took one hundred and forty-eight days to get there. But she was not the first Shaw Savill ship to plop an

By courtesy of the Shaw Savill Line

s.s. *Kumara* (1899), a three-masted, barquentine-rigged cargo-ship used for transport work in the Boer War. In the First World War she served under the liner-requisition scheme

32

s.s. *Maimoa* (1920), a coal-burning, twin-screwed cargo-ship of 11,291 gross tons

By courtesy of the Shaw Savill Line

The *Gothic*, in which the Queen and Prince Philip sailed for their tour of New Zealand and Australia in 1953 (p. 43)

The *Laurentic*, one of Shaw Savill's latest refrigerated cargo-liners

anchor in New Zealand waters. The *Avalanche*, 753 tons, sailing over two months later, arrived in Auckland after ninety-five days on September 27th, 1858, some three weeks before *Chieftain*.

Shaw and Savill obviously had a flair for publicity. The mere mention of "goldfields" was sufficient to attract attention; and they lost no time in telling the Under-Secretary for the Colonies that they were in the New Zealand trade and available to take Government dispatches and ship letters.

They also showed a sure touch in selecting their own House Flag—the first and discarded New Zealand 'national' flag. It had the red cross of St George on a white ground and, in the upper quarter next to the hoist, another St George's cross, this time on blue ground with a white star in each quarter. It had been approved by Maori chiefs in 1834. The Maoris had adopted it, and so had ships sailing in New Zealand waters. It had fluttered gaily until the signing of the Treaty of Waitangi in 1840, when the Union Jack became the Colony's official flag, and merchant ships flew the Red Ensign.

The partners snapped up the discard, perhaps with an eye to flaunting their challenge to Robert Henderson and James Galbraith, two Scots operating the Albion Line to New Zealand, whose House Flag was the reversed French tricolour with the Union Jack in the white section. The former New Zealand flag had a touch of the White Ensign of the Royal Navy about it, and evidently Shaw and Savill felt that anything with a look of the Royal Navy was more than a match for a Frenchified piece of bunting.

There was, however, no plagiarism about the Albion flag. Henderson had been in shipping since he was nineteen, one of four brothers from the greystone village of Pittenweem, in Fifeshire, who had formed

3

Patrick Henderson and Co. in 1834. The Hendersons
sent their ships to many countries, and when the
Crimean War broke out in 1854 they chartered two
vessels to the French Government as troopers—at
twice the rate paid by the British. The French were
so satisfied with the Hendersons' service that they
agreed to the Scottish ships flying the tricolour with
the Union Jack in the white section. Robert Henderson
promptly adopted it as his House Flag, while agreeing
to the French request to reverse the tricolour to avoid
confusion.

Competition between the two companies was keen.
Ashore they sought bigger cargoes, more passengers;
afloat the masters bet top-hats on the fastest passages.
Perhaps the pace was too hot for Willis, Gann and
Co., who dropped out of the New Zealand trade during
the sixties.

But Shaw had only a short time to enjoy success with
his partner. Six years after they had set up in business
he died in November 1864, when he was only forty-one.
Savill went into partnership with James Temple, an
experienced merchant, and he did not retire until 1892.
When he died in April 1911, aged seventy-four, he
was a millionaire.

Few years lay ahead of Robert Henderson, last of the
Henderson brothers. He died in May 1868, aged
fifty-seven, and Galbraith, his partner from Strathaven,
inherited the business—and the House Flag.

For the next fourteen years Savill and Temple
competed with Galbraith, until, in 1882, with the
arrival of refrigeration, they amalgamated the two
companies, which became Shaw Savill and Albion
under the chairmanship of another Scot who was to
be raised to the peerage from the Commons—Lord
Ritchie—with a fellow-Scot, John Potter, as manager.

This was the first change in the ownership of the

two companies, Sanderson reflected. Others began with the turn of the century. After 1902 Shaw Savill and Albion became closely associated with the White Star Line, through which it was brought into the sphere of the International Mercantile Marine Company, and his father began to take an interest in its affairs. Several ships were now owned jointly by Shaw Savill and White Star, and in 1905 the two companies bought a large proportion of the shares of Thompson's Aberdeen Line, which changed from a family to a public company with his father as chairman.

Five years later Sir John Ellerman bought Shaw Savill shares, and a large measure of control, and other shares were held by White Star. In 1911 his father became chairman of Shaw Savill.

This regime continued until 1927. Then Lord Kylsant bought control of White Star, and in April 1928 acquired Sir John Ellerman's Shaw Savill holding. His father gave up the chairmanship in June.

The next change was in 1931. Lord Kylsant, who had varied interests, was convicted of issuing a false prospectus for one of his many companies and sentenced to twelve months' imprisonment. John Macmillan became chairman for two years, until Furness, Withy and Co. took up a one-third holding in Shaw Savill in 1933. Lord Essendon, who had begun life as an office-boy in Hartlepool with Furness Withy, went into the chair, and in 1936 bought the Shaw Savill shares held by White Star. When he died in June 1944 he was succeeded by Walter Warwick, chairman of Houlder Bros and Co., and other companies, until 1947.

Now, Sanderson told himself as he strolled back from the garden to his study, he had the responsibilities of chairman. He wondered what Shaw and Savill, and Henderson and Galbraith, would have thought of the men who had followed them and the ships they had built. Maybe they had kept an eye on things from wherever all good shipowners go after life.

They would certainly be interested in the ships . . . the *Margaret Galbraith*, 899 tons, and the first iron ship designed and built for the New Zealand trade in 1868 . . . the 1058-ton iron clipper *Crusader*, built in 1869 and claimed as one of the fastest and most beautiful sailing-ships of all time, making the record time of sixty-five days from Lyttelton to the English Channel in 1877, and earning her keep for the company for just on thirty years.

There had been so many others. A big step forward had been *Arawa* and *Tainui* after the amalgamation of the two companies. They had engines and two funnels, four masts, clipper stems, and fine lines. They averaged fifteen knots, and went round the world in a little more than seventy days.

Then, in 1893, there had been the first *Gothic*, nearly 8000 tons, the first twin-screw ship to sail to New Zealand, and the biggest seen in the Port of London for four years . . . the *Delphic*, just over 8000 tons, and in 1897 the biggest ship on the New Zealand run.

With the new century, in 1902 and 1903, came the sister ships, the first *Athenic*, *Corinthic*, and *Ionic*, 12,200 tons . . . between 1909 and 1911 the *Rangatira*, *Waimana*, *Pakeha*, and *Zealandic*, 10,000 tons, began their service. In 1917 there was the *Mahana*, the company's first turbine steamer, 11,796 tons . . . and in 1928 the first diesel-engine ships *Zealandic*, *Coptic*, *Taranaki*, and *Karamea*, 11,300 tons, with a speed around fifteen knots. Then in 1934 and 1935 the motor-ships, *Waipawa*, *Waiwera*, and *Wairangi* and their cruiser sterns, costing £1 million for the three, and claimed as the finest of their type in the world.

Just before the War, in July 1938, the 26,463-ton

Dominion Monarch was launched, pride of the Shaw
Savill fleet, carrying more passengers and more cargo
than any of the company's other ships; she had four
screws and a service speed of nineteen and a half
knots, which meant she could collect records with
ease, and she began a new return service to Wellington
by way of Cape Town, Durban, and the Australian
ports.

The "four originals", as Sanderson sometimes
thought of Shaw, Savill, Henderson, and Galbraith,
would have delighted in all these ships, and not the
least in *Dominion Monarch*, which could have swung
the tiny *Chieftain* aboard with her electric winches
and accommodated her as easily as Gargantua filling
his maw.

Yet, primarily, they were businessmen, and however
much the lines of a ship might please their eyes it
was the credit balances in their account-books which
warmed their hearts. In return for cash they aimed to
give good value and the best possible conditions for
their passengers—the "early settlers" in New Zealand,
who were to become almost legendary.

A voyage across the world a century ago was an
adventure and something of a gamble in the small
wooden and iron ships, and there were often times
when hope rather than confidence was at the helm.
Land was out of sight for months once the ships set
out from Britain, made for South America, crossed
to the Cape of Good Hope, and, sailing far south
before the prevailing winds, skirted Tasmania and
slowly made their way to the Land of the Long White
Cloud. There was monotony and hardship; food was
dull, fresh water scarce. Passengers provided their own
entertainment. The masters were feudal, the crews
tough and hard, and the most popular person aboard
was often the surgeon, who added the work of purser

to his medical duties. The speed of the mails was the speed of the ships, and sometimes half a year went by before relatives in Britain received word of safe arrivals after the ships had made their homeward run across the South Pacific, round the Horn, and up the long drag of the Atlantic.

Neither Shaw nor Savill went to New Zealand, but they believed in its future, and with their flair for publicity sponsored a book, *New Zealand, the Land of Promise and Resources*, which gave an account of the Colony and "hints about ships". Fares were not low, judged on the current value of money, and the £60 paid for a single first-class cabin, to be furnished by the passenger, was a tidy sum. There were inducements, however, and these included the free grant of forty acres to all who paid their own full fares, offered by the New Zealand Company which had been founded in England to acquire land from the Maoris and establish British settlers on it. Passengers were expected to observe certain regulations introduced by the two companies: the sale of liquor dependent on doctor's orders; the segregation of married couples and children, and of single men and women.

The flow of settlers was steady, developing periodically into successive waves. One of the most notable began after Julius Vogel, the New Zealand Treasurer, borrowed £12 million in 1870 to develop the Colony. It reached a peak between June 1874 and May 1875, when ninety-three ships took out nearly thirty-two thousand settlers—English, Scots, Irish, and some Germans and Scandinavians—who paid between £12 and £13 each.

The next surge of immigration began in 1904, its stream aided by the arrival of refrigeration and electricity in the new steamships. Twenty years later, in 1926, people were on the move again from Britain to New Zealand, and a fourth wave began in 1946, when distant pastures looked green to a blitzed, war-weary, and rationed people. It was continuing, and could be expected to continue, and this was one of the reasons, Sanderson reflected, why one-third of the berths in the new ship to be built in Belfast would be earmarked for such settlers.

Passengers and cargo—these were the essentials upon which the "four originals" had based their business. There was to be a development which was to multiply both far beyond the most imaginative dreams: refrigeration, which was to change and improve the daily fare of a great many people in the world. Galbraith immediately grasped its possibilities.

After successful Australian and American experiments he equipped the 1320-ton clipper iron ship *Dunedin* with refrigerating machinery and insulating chambers, and sent her from Glasgow to Port Chalmers. She was loaded, after one or two setbacks, with 5000 carcasses of mutton and lamb, and arrived in London 98 days later on May 26th, 1882, after an eventful voyage. The sails were set alight several times by sparks from the refrigeration plant's funnel. The master was once nearly frozen to death while looking for a fault in the refrigeration ventilation.

At Smithfield, London's great meat market, the shipment was snapped up at an average price of $6\frac{1}{2}d$. a lb., nearly double its value in New Zealand. From that moment New Zealand was assured of a promising future.

Refrigeration meant so many things: to shipowners a two-way traffic for cargo as well as passengers; for New Zealand and Australia a steady development of their farming land; for Britain a cheap food policy aiding industrial expansion—and vital supplies of food in the two wars that lay ahead.

It also meant the amalgamation of Shaw Savill with Albion. Within five months of the *Dunedin*'s voyage, and with the knowledge that New Zealand farmers were demanding refrigerated steamers to replace sailing-ships, and that the New Zealand Shipping Company would shortly be in the field, the two companies combined as Shaw Savill and Albion.

This was history, and Galbraith, who had contributed an important link, had lived just long enough to glimpse the future. He died two years later, in 1884.

History . . . the two companies were part of the warp and woof of New Zealand history. Shaw Savill had carried men and women to her gold rush in 1861 . . . soldiers to the second Maori war in the sixties, 500 men of the 14th Regiment in the *Robert Lowe*, and 300 troops in the *Sea King*. The Maori war . . . the Boer War, when an earlier *Waiwera* sailed on October 1st, 1899, for Cape Town with the first contingent of New Zealand troops ever to fight abroad. She and other ships returned with South African sand as ballast, which still provides a pleasant beach at Oriental Bay in Wellington.

Then the First World War, of which Sanderson had his own memories. Gallipoli . . . the Anzacs . . . they had been landed by *Athenic*, *Arawa*, and *Waimana*. And Flanders, where he had largely served . . . ship after ship had brought New Zealand and Australian reinforcements to mud and slaughter, and taken the fortunate ones home again . . . and helped to feed Britain.

The Second World War, when the company lost thirteen of its fleet of twenty-six . . . the *Tairoa*, sunk by the *Graf Spee*, most of her crew put aboard the supply tanker *Altmark*, but rescued from a Norwegian fjord by H.M.S. *Cossack* with the greeting which went round the world—"The Navy's here" . . . the *Doric Star*, also sunk by the *Graf Spee*, but giving the Admiralty a vital clue which led to the Battle of River Plate . . . the *Jervis Bay*, belting at full speed straight at the guns of the pocket battleship *Admiral Scheer*, saving a convoy while being sunk and losing several men, including the gallant Captain Fogarty Fegen, R.N., awarded a posthumous Victoria Cross . . . the Malta convoy of August 1942, when *Wairangi*, *Waimarama*, and *Empire Hope* were bombed and sunk. Losses . . . losses . . . but the Second New Zealand Expeditionary Force reinforced throughout its campaigns in the Middle East, the Western Desert, and Italy . . . thousands of Australian and New Zealand airmen landed in Britain to fly with the Royal Air Force and the Fleet Air Arm . . . hundreds to serve in the Royal Navy. All pieces in the broad mosaic of history.

And it was possible that another bright piece would yet be added . . . a Royal Tour of the Commonwealth in one of the company's new ships, *Gothic*. Twice she had been made ready . . . in 1951, last year, when King George, Queen Elizabeth, and Princess Margaret were to travel in her to New Zealand and Australia . . . but the King's health had caused a cancellation . . . and earlier this year, in February 1952, when *Gothic* waited at Mombasa for Princess Elizabeth and Prince Philip, who were to carry out the tour for the King and Queen. The visit had never been carried out. The King had died, and the young Princess had flown back to London with her husband to begin her reign.

Now . . . July 1952 . . . the future tour was still postponed indefinitely . . . a piece still to be added to the mosaic. Well, the new ship would probably make history, too, certainly for Shaw Savill and perhaps for shipping . . . but what kind of history? A story of success? Or were the Jonahs right, and was it 'dangerous' to build a liner with engines aft? Sanderson did not think so, neither did Cameron. Nor Swan.

Sanderson's light was out by ten as usual that night . . . it had been a satisfying, interesting day.

CHAPTER FOUR

"*I name this Ship* . . ."

THAT bright piece of mosaic—the use of *Gothic* for the Royal Tour of New Zealand and Australia—did become part of Shaw Savill history. But early in November 1953, when she was preparing to sail in a fresh white coat for Jamaica, where the Queen and Prince Philip were to board her, it seemed possible that a black chip might be added too.

Sanderson told Harland and Wolff to stop work on the new ship, No. 1498, in the Belfast yards.

This startling directive resulted from uncertainties over meeting the safety regulations of the Ministry of Transport, with which all ships built in Britain must comply.

It appeared that if the regulations were to be observed the ship would not be able to run to a strict timetable, which was to be fundamental to her service. She would therefore be uneconomic.

From a layman's point of view the uncertainties were technical. They concerned side-damage stability, and the degree of list or loll the ship might develop in the event of a collision. If a sharp list, it might become impossible to lower the lifeboats on the side opposite to the list. But, by the redistribution of freshwater ballast in the ship, she could be kept in a sufficiently upright position, at least temporarily, to allow all lifeboats to be lowered safely.

The Ministry's regulations indicated that the amount

of freshwater ballast which it had been proposed to use was insufficient to keep the ship level in the event of severe damage. Yet, if more ballast were provided, refuelling in ports would become a protracted business and completely disrupt the timetable.

One of the engineering objections to building a passenger-ship with engines aft had been this very problem of stability—of preventing her being bow- or stern-heavy, or listing either to port or starboard. Cameron had overcome this possibility by designing a hull with a system of tanks placed in such a manner that, when filled with either fuel-oil or distilled water as ballast, they would keep the ship upright— in other words, her stability or trim would be constant.

This system meant that tanks emptied of fuel-oil burned by the boiler fires would be refilled with distilled water (sea water would cause corrosion), and the trim maintained.

A distillation plant, capable of producing 300 tons of distilled water a day, had been ordered to provide ballast and also to meet the flow required by the boilers and by domestic needs.

Equally essential as having water for ballast was emptying it from the tanks before refuelling; and, since it would be fouled by a residue of fuel-oil, an oily-water separator was needed for purification. Provision had been made for a separator capable of 'cleaning' 100 tons of oily water an hour.

The system of tanks in No. 1498 provided for 1500 tons of distilled-water ballast. But, to meet the regulations of the Ministry of Transport, a ballast of 2500 tons was required.

The extra 1000 tons meant that more tanks would be needed, and space would have to be found for them by redesigning the ship's layout. This water would also have to be purified, causing the ship to remain a longer time in ports.

The problem was resolved at a meeting on November 12th, 1953, when Sanderson, with Lockhart, Craig, and others, met Baillie, Cameron, and Pounder.

They agreed to provide the extra ballast by reducing the size of the crew recreation room and extending the tanks to the sides of the ship; and to increase the rate of purifying the oily water to 500 tons an hour by installing two oily-water separators each with a capacity of 250 tons an hour. Thus the Ministry's regulations could be met, and the stipulated 2500 tons of water ballast cleaned and pumped clear in five or six hours. She could keep to her strict timetable.

Work began again on ship No. 1498.

Sanderson and his fellow directors were enthusiastic over Cameron's design. The ship was finely modelled, with a curved rounded bow, a cruiser stern, and streamlined bridge.

The bridge was midships, the engines aft, and there were eight decks for the passengers, ranging from the sports deck on the top of the ship to B deck. Between them lay the sun, lounge, promenade, main, restaurant, and A decks. Cabins for passengers were on six of the decks, each cabin accommodating from one to six berths. On the lounge deck were the majority of the public rooms—the forward lounge, the smoke-room, the cinema lounge, the Tavern, the writing-room and library. Above them on the sun deck were the children's recreation room and play area, and the infants' play-room and play deck. There were two restaurants, one forward for 390 people, the other aft for 192, with the kitchens between them. There would be plenty of space for 1160 passengers. Fares would vary according to the position of the cabin as well as the number of berths.

The important innovation was air-conditioning in all passenger cabins, the two dining saloons, the cinema lounge, the two small hospitals—one for men, the other for women—the shop, the hairdressing saloons, and in the recreation rooms for the crew, and in some crew cabins. This meant that the ship would have more air-conditioning for her passengers than any other afloat. It would, however, not be installed on the bridge or in the quarters of the navigating officers.

Another innovation was a single, wide central alleyway on every deck, instead of two either side of the ship, which would simplify the passengers' route to their cabins as well as to muster-stations and lifeboats in the event of emergency.

Other new features included the covering of the bulkheads, or walls, with laminated plywood to do away with periodical painting of woodwork, and the fitting of stabilizers to prevent or reduce rolling in heavy seas. There were to be two swimming-pools, with dressing-rooms, a medium-sized one on the sun deck, the other, larger, on the lower deck in the bowels of the ship.

With the funnel at the stern there should be little if any smoke and fumes blowing over the decks, except, perhaps, in a following wind. But to ensure as far as possible that smoke could be kept clear of the decks, no matter what quarter the wind, experiments were carried out by the Aerodynamics Division of the National Physical Laboratory at Teddington.

A 1/64th-inch scale model of the ship above the water-line was placed in a wind-tunnel, and steam was used for a smoke-plume. Several funnel profiles were tried, and winds of twenty to thirty knots simulated while the ship was estimated to be travelling at ten and eighteen and a half knots. Photographs were taken of the steam-plume.

From these experiments the most effective funnel profile was selected, and photographs showed that its plume blew free and above all parts of the model in a following wind, or a wind from any other direction for that matter. The laboratory's recommendation was adopted, and the only subsequent addition was the fitting of a fan inside the funnel casing which sent the smoke and gases still higher into the air and above the ship.

All these points were watched over carefully by Captain Lockhart, the Line's marine superintendent, who had naturally taken a leading part at every stage of the planning, and worked in close association with Sanderson. Lockhart had seen many changes and improvements in ships since he had first gone to sea with the Line in November 1916 as a fifteen-year-old cadet. Born at Leigh-on-Sea, Essex, and educated at the now defunct St George's College, Kingsway, London, he served in several ships until January 1938, when he became Shaw Savill's superintendent in Glasgow. During the War, although stationed in Liverpool, he also continued to keep an eye on the Scottish port. After the War he was transferred to London as assistant to Captain John Wilson, the Line's marine superintendent, whom he succeeded in January 1950.

Lockhart travelled regularly to Belfast as work on the new ship proceeded steadily. Two hundred and fifty firms throughout Britain now had contracts to supply her many requirements.

Mrs Ainley and Mrs Errington Keville planned and chose the decorations for the public rooms and the cabins—mock-ups of which were built in Belfast to ensure that every foot of space was used to the best advantage.

Sanderson had to make two essential decisions: who

should be invited to launch No. 1498, and what name
should be given to the ship?

His thoughts turned to *Gothic* and the reports that
all was going well on the Royal Tour. He wondered
whether the Queen might accept an invitation; no
reigning monarch had yet launched a merchant ship—
a warship, yes, but no passenger-ship. He decided to
write to the Queen's Secretary, Sir Michael Adeane,
to discover whether the suggestion might be considered.

Sir Michael replied from Australia—yes, the Queen
would be pleased to launch the new ship.

And now—the name. Should memories of great
Shaw Savill ships of the past be revived, like *Crusader*?
Or should it be . . . *Southern Cross*, the constellation
which both New Zealand and Australia incorporated
in their national flags, which had blinked down on so
much of the company's history, and under which the
new ship would spend two-thirds of her voyages?

Sanderson cabled three names to Sir Michael
Adeane for submission to the Queen. Sir Michael
replied that Her Majesty agreed to *Southern Cross*,
which Sanderson had placed at the head of the list.

It was a choice that was to meet with only one
dissentient—Archbishop Owen of New Zealand, whose
objection was that the Melanesian Mission to the Gilbert
and Ellice Islands named its ships *Southern Cross*.

A final point remained to be agreed with Sir Michael
and Harland and Wolff—the date of the launching.
This was fixed for August 17th, 1954.

By now to the din of the riveters in Belfast, sweet
music to thousands of men in the shipyards, 1498 was
fast taking shape. The great hull reared high between
the gantries, and superstructure above the promenade
deck, including the bridge, was being added. The
davits, where the fifteen lifeboats would rest, looked
like so many cobras arching to strike.

Photos by courtesy of Harland and Wolff

"To the din of the riveters . . . 1498 was fast taking shape" (p. 48)

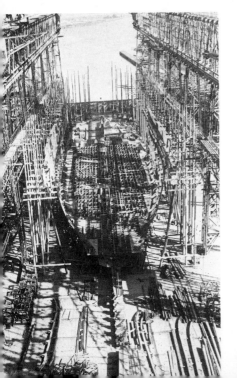

The building of *Southern Cross*

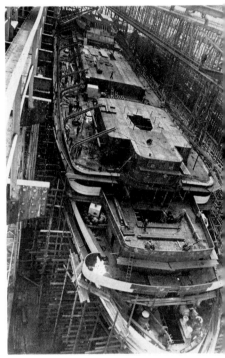

49

"The great hull reared high between the gantries" (p. 48)

Photos by courtesy of Harland and Wolff

As August drew near, the painters got to work. Rusty steel became black to the water-line, light grey covered the hull, pale green, or eau-de-nil, the superstructure. These colours were a radical change from the Line's traditional black and buff (which were retained for the funnel) and were adopted after the success of painting *Gothic* white for the Royal Tour.

The lettering "Southern Cross" appeared on both sides of the bow, and on the stern; and the Line's House Flag, chosen nearly a century before by Shaw, was brushed high on the bow.

From Leadenhall Street some four hundred invitations were sent to official guests to watch the Queen make merchant-shipping history. Special trains were booked to run from London, and the Belfast ferry was reserved for the trip across the Irish Channel.

Tuesday, August 17th, 1954, dawned to grey skies, drizzling rain that fell more heavily as the morning wore on, and half a gale.

The Queen was at Balmoral Castle and was to fly in a Viking of the Queen's Flight from Dyce to Aldergrove, some fourteen miles from Queen's Island, where 1498 stood in No. Two slipway and where the yards were bedecked and ships to the smallest collier dressed over-all.

The weather was as bad in Scotland as in Ulster, take-off was late, and there was low cloud and rain. Meanwhile along the route from Aldergrove to the shipyards men, women, and children, swathed in raincoats and gripping umbrellas, began to wait for a glimpse of the Queen.

At Queen's Island the official guests made their way to the tarpaulin-covered stand facing the ship, and 7000 shipyard workers, lucky in a ballot, with their wives and families, massed in the slipway in the drenching rain.

4

The launching was scheduled for 1.15 P.M., and word was brought to Sanderson and Sir Frederick Rebbeck, who at one period wondered whether the flight could be made, that the Queen would be at least fifteen, perhaps thirty minutes late. Shortly before one o'clock James Colville, the assistant yard manager, spoke to Sanderson. He said that all the blocks holding the ship in position had been knocked away. It would not be safe to delay the launch for more than half an hour after the scheduled time. Sanderson realized that if the Queen had not arrived by 1.45 P.M. the ship would have to be launched without her. It was a worrying phase.

The Queen, however, had already landed at Aldergrove, and been greeted by Lord Wakehurst, Governor of Northern Ireland, and Lady Wakehurst. She had also met Lord Rathcavan, Lieutenant for County Antrim, Lord Brookeborough, the Prime Minister, and Lady Brookeborough.

At the slipway the visitors were dry under the tarpaulin; outside, the black bulbs of hundreds of umbrellas glistened in the rain. Miles away, in Dublin, the Anti-Partition Association paraded in front of the British Embassy, protesting at the Queen's visit to Belfast. Eight thousand Ulster regular police and special constabulary were on duty along the 180-mile Ulster-Eire border, in quiet country roads, and in Belfast itself.

The Queen, due at the slipway at 1 P.M., left Aldergrove fifteen minutes behind schedule, attended by Sir Michael Adeane. Police cleared the road to the slipway, and once the Queen's car reached the main Antrim-Belfast road the chauffeur increased speed as the car shot along and the Queen waved to groups on the roadside.

A fast drive through Belfast streets, with other cars in the convoy now well behind, and the Royal Standard

arrived at Harland and Wolff's on time, with the lost
fifteen minutes regained. Sir Frederick and Sanderson
were presented by Lord Glentoran, Lieutenant for
Belfast, there was a short drive to the slipway, and the
Queen stepped out of her car to a burst of cheering
and the National Anthem, played by the band of the
Royal Inniskilling Fusiliers. Then, under the shelter
of an umbrella held by Rebbeck, she mounted the
launching platform.

This was the moment for which Sanderson had
planned, and he smiled as he noticed that the Queen
was wearing over a floral frock a coat which almost
exactly matched the pale green of the ship's superstructure. He tried to forget about a pool of rainwater
overhead in a slightly bellying canvas as a seventeen-
year-old apprentice shipwright, John Collins, presented
the Queen with a bouquet of lilies of the valley,
orchids, and roses.

A pause while Sir Frederick waited for the clock to
show exactly 1.15 P.M. and explained to the Queen
the launching mechanism; and then, with Sanderson
on the Queen's left, they stood before the microphones,
the great bow of the ship towering above them.

The traditional phrase spoken by the Queen: "I
name this ship *Southern Cross* . . . May God protect
her and all who sail in her" . . . a bottle of wine
smashing and splintering against steel, a hissing and
dribbling of white foam . . . and a moment later the
ship beginning to move . . . an inch, two inches . . .
a foot . . . a yard . . . and she was away to a burst of
cheering and cacophony of hooters.

There are few sights as thrilling as a ship gliding
down a slipway, a mass of tailored steel, until she is
cushioned and cosseted by the sea. Now rusty chains
uncoiled, ready to hold *Southern Cross* steady when
she had ended her run, rattling billowing patches of

brownish dust . . . a steady rumble developed while
she slid with mounting speed along the wooden,
greased runway. She entered the water, and a wave
broke from her stern . . . and as buoyancy lifted her so
she dipped a curtsy . . . to those who had planned for
her, designed her, built her . . . and to the gentle yet
firm gloved hand that had sent her on the first few
hundred yards of the many thousands of miles to come.
Tugs soon held her surely, and began inching her to
her berth.

The Queen watched this shepherding; then turning
in a full circle she smiled and waved to the thousands
who cheered her as they stood in the pelting rain,
and waved again as she left the platform and drove
away to an official luncheon.

There, before the guests were seated, Sir Frederick
Rebbeck presented her with a decanter and glasses
for the royal yacht *Britannia*. Later, when he proposed
the toast of "The Queen", he thanked her for inter-
rupting her holiday, and recalled that she had last
visited Belfast in 1946 as Princess Elizabeth to launch
the aircraft-carrier *Eagle*. Now, he added, she had
become the first reigning British monarch to launch
a merchant ship, a ship "revolutionary" in design.

"Never has a British merchant ship had a more
auspicious launching," he said.

Sanderson endorsed Sir Frederick's thanks, and
mentioned the Royal Tour and the *Gothic*.

"My colleagues and I in the Shaw Savill Company,"
he continued, "are determined not to let the past be
an excuse for resting on our oars, but we shall regard
it as a spur to the future development of our trade
with those great members of the Commonwealth,
Australia, New Zealand, and South Africa, which we
regard as our birthright, as our privilege, and as our
duty."

Sir Frederick had another presentation for the Queen
—two inscribed gold salvers commemorating the
launching.

"Our great shipbuilding industry may well take
pride in the *Southern Cross*," said the Queen, after
she had thanked Sir Frederick and Sanderson for their
welcome, and expressed her pleasure at the salvers
and the glassware.

"She is entirely new and original, and while we are
deeply confident in our traditional skill, I think it is
right that we should give the lead in new departures
of modern design. I congratulate all those who have
planned and built her, as well as the company which
has ordered her to replace some of the losses suffered
in the War, and to keep pace with the changing
conditions of service.

"I have recently travelled many thousands of miles
in the *Gothic*, and in her I have been to many of the
ports to which *Southern Cross* will sail. This new ship
will encircle the world four times a year. What nobler
cause could she serve than to bring those countries
of the Commonwealth and Empire, and their peoples,
closer together."

The Queen toasted "this noble addition to our
Merchant Navy, the prosperity of the *Southern Cross*,
and the health and happiness of all who serve in her."

After members of the two companies had been
presented, including Baillie, Pounder, Cameron, Lockhart, Craig, and Sir David Aitchison, master of the
Gothic and already named first master of *Southern
Cross*, the Queen left Queen's Island just two hours
after the ship had entered the water, and made a more
leisurely drive through lined streets and roads to
Aldergrove. It was still raining when her Viking took
off on the return flight to Dyce.

Six months later, in January 1955, *Southern Cross*

was handed over to Shaw Savill by Harland and Wolff, which Sanderson regarded as "remarkably quick" delivery.

Shortly after her launching her "machinery installation"—as the technicians say—was lowered into position: a twin-screw arrangement of geared turbines with three high-pressure boilers. The installation was in three watertight compartments—a boiler-room, engine-room, and generator-room.

The propelling machinery was built by Harland and Wolff, and consisted of a two-shaft arrangement of compound, condensing double-reduction geared steam turbines developing 20,000 shaft horsepower at 120 revolutions per minute of the propeller, sufficient to maintain a speed of twenty knots. The main boiler system consisted of three Yarrow-type boilers designed for a pressure of 550 lb. per square inch at the steam drum, with an aggregate maximum continuous evaporation of 180,000 lb. of steam per hour, and a controlled superheat temperature of 800° F. In the generator-room there were six 600-k.w. 220-volt Allen generators driven by six eight-cylinder diesel engines.

As Craig was later to tell the Institute of Marine Engineers, when commenting on the complications of siting the machinery in the stern, moving from midships the machinery spaces from which the life-blood of a ship flows—the light, heat, and power—was rather like moving the human heart to the head. All the blood to and from it had now to flow along a restricted neck-passage. Numerous pipe services, ballast, boiler deisel-fuel filling, bilge, and steam heating had to pass from the engine-room through all intervening machinery spaces to the forward end of the ship.

To reduce rolling by *Southern Cross* to a minimum in bad weather two Denny-Brown stabilizers were

fitted. This stabilizing system consisted of two fins
or hydrofoils, one projecting from either side of the
ship. Each fin measured twelve feet long by six feet
six inches in breadth, and had an area of seventy-
eight square feet. Their control was an electric switch
on the bridge.

The work in Belfast went on speedily, the funnel
was mounted, and also the mast, the subject of a
number of designs. And while hundreds of details
were dealt with from the officers' and the crew's
quarters to the kitchens, Mrs Ainley and Mrs Keville
watched the public rooms develop colour and comfort.

Comfort had to be combined with utility, and as
Southern Cross would be spending much of her life
in tropical waters there could be no heavy opulence
which could become oppressive in humid weather.
Materials were chosen to give an impression of airiness,
and a considerable amount of wood panelling was
used on stairways and in the public rooms for
homeliness.

These rooms were magnificently large, and where
possible stretched the entire beam of the ship. The
forward lounge had windows on three sides and gave
an illusion of being circular. In the centre were slender
pillars of satin-finished stainless steel which suggested
a separate room inside the lounge, with its large, oval
hand-made carpet of deep pile in wine and white.
Pastels were used for the colour motif, and there were
printed fabrics in smoke blue, daphne, pink, and
white. The deck was covered with Ruboleum in pastel
blue and black, and these colours were repeated in the
upholstery of chairs for card-tables. Decorative glass
screens at the forward end, sandblasted and etched
with figures of Australian and New Zealand birds,
broke the expanse of the room, which, at night,
had its ceiling floodlit from bowls on bases of Nigerian

wood bearing the Southern Cross constellation. As the room was also intended for church services, an altar was concealed behind panelling. Aft, on the port side, windows looked into the adjoining writing-room; in the corresponding section on the bow side, but hidden from the lounge, was the library.

The motif of the smoke-room amidships was again circular. It was panelled by silver-grey veneers cut from the elm piles of London's old Waterloo Bridge which once spanned the Thames, and dark walnut. Red hide banquette seating with grey piping and buttons skirted the walls and windows. Tables with reversible tops for card-players had comfortable armchairs, and easy chairs were tub-type. The circular ceiling was stepped up into a shallow dome, its lighting concealed. Murals of the arms of Australia, New Zealand, and South Africa were in oils and enamels, painted by William Morris, in three corners. The fourth corner provided a bar.

The cinema lounge, further aft, was rectangular, with a height of seventeen feet and a balcony over the forward end. A multi-purpose room—used for dancing and concerts as well as a cinema and lounge—it had a stage cloaked by a curtain designed by Miss Doris Zinkeisen. Chadwell tapestry in red, green, and yellow was used for settees and easy chairs, which also had loose covers of old bleached linen in green and rose. There was a long bar under the balcony. The sloping floor meant that chairs could be placed at graduated heights to give a good view of the stage.

In the Tavern, between the cinema lounge and the stern, the thirty-foot-long bar with a bright red top was a natural and expected feature looking out to 'Bierkeller' seating to encourage intimate groups, and to a dance-floor. The walls were covered in a printed green and white plastic, the ceiling in natural pine.

Doors aft opened on to decks, and on the starboard side tall windows overlooked the sea.

Two decks below, the aft and forward restaurants were cut off from daylight, but brightened by colour and design and frameless, toughened glass etched with flowers of Britain and her Commonwealth sister countries. In the forward restaurant Perspex panels showed moths, butterflies, and birds designed by Dr Arthur Fleischman, and in both restaurants there were relief carvings in limewood by Howard Bate, representing the sporting life of Australia and New Zealand.

The cabins were in two shades of colour—blue or cream—and those without portholes were given a circular light to be switched on automatically shortly before 7 A.M. and increasing in intensity to suggest the rising sun. Every cabin had hot and cold running water, some a shower and lavatory; and the mock-ups in Belfast made certain there was no wasted room, but adequate wardrobes for every passenger and space under the beds for travelling-cases.

There were two lifts, one from A deck to the cinema lounge, the other from the lower deck and the swimming-pool to the lounge deck. And as for deck space, there was a total of 42,000 square feet, or over 35 square feet for every passenger, with a sports deck of nearly 5000 square feet.

Decorations and colour schemes were designed to give an atmosphere of homeliness and leisure; and this was to be reflected, as voyages and the years began to tick by, in her reputation for being a 'friendly' ship.

As the date of her handing over to the Shaw Savill Line approached, of her trials and also her maiden voyage, her executive staff was appointed. They were the Line's most senior and experienced officers, all determined to make sure, as far as lay in their power, that the new ship would be a success.

The master, Captain Sir David Aitchison, K.C.V.O., commodore of the company's fleet, had been knighted by the Queen just before she left *Gothic* at Aden at the end of the Royal Tour. Tall, kindly, shrewd, he invariably called his officers "laddie"; he was sixty-three, with two years to serve before retiring.

His decision to go to sea when a boy of seventeen had a touch of the story-book about it, for he had been born in Sunderland, County Durham, and grown up in an atmosphere in which it seemed that all the men he knew of had been to sea, were going to sea, or were at sea. His parents were not enthusiastic. His father was a papermaker, and felt that a man should make his career ashore; but there were four cousins who were all ship's masters and had sailed the seven seas.

And the sea—he had only to look out over a meadow from his bedroom window every morning to watch its changing moods; and at week-ends when he could forget about school he would wander round the Sunderland docks, eyeing the steamers and sailing-ships and dreaming of the day when he would be old enough to sign on. It was natural that he should enlist the aid of one of the cousins when his schooldays ended, and together they plodded round to interview all the shipping firms in the town. They were met with shakes of the head, for few jobs were open in 1908. The following year, however, he was signed on as an apprentice by V. T. Thompson and Co., who owned seven tramps, and off to sea he went, working as a seaman, but taking his meals in his cabin, for he was well below the officers' salt.

Four years later, at the end of 1913, he had his certificate as a second mate and signed on with Andrew

Weir and Co. as third officer in *Gifford*, a tramp running
between Galveston, in Texas, and Hamburg, carrying
grain and cotton. The ship was in Hamburg at the
beginning of August 1914, when the Kaiser was busy
tearing up scraps of paper. She nearly got away from
Cuxhaven before war was declared, but she was
stopped by the Germans and sent back to Hamburg
on August 3rd, and the following day Aitchison and
his shipmates found themselves in hulks, and prisoners
of war.

Aitchison was twenty-two, and he was to be twenty-
six before he left an internment camp at Ruhrleben.
They were dull, dragging years, but he became friendly
with a Fellow of Caius College, Cambridge, a mathe-
matical physicist, and took up the study of mathematics
under his guidance. He also planned ahead. Once the
War was over, he would not return to sea, but study
mathematics at Caius. It was a good plan, but when
the time arrived for him to return to England he
discovered that, among the many changes caused by
the War, money had no longer the same value. His
savings would not go far at Cambridge. He applied
for a grant to assist him, but he was not eligible.
Nevertheless he did go up to Caius. Money continued
to be a worry, and the mathematics was complicated.
He stayed for the term and began to find himself out
of his depth. When he was handed a book on pure
geometry with the nonchalant comment that it was
something he could read before breakfast the old
sailor in him said, "Hell, I'm going back to sea." He
did not return from vacation.

Others went back to pure geometry, but he was
fourth officer in Shaw Savill's *Wahehe*, and between
April 1919 and March 1931 he worked his way up to
chief officer. An inquiry made in 1926, when he was
two years married and there was a seamen's strike,

brought an answer out of the blue. He had sought a job ashore and made a number of unsuccessful applications. Then five years later he was invited to become towage master to the Leith Salvage and Towage Company, near Edinburgh. He was not keen, but a shore job was a shore job, and money was to be made in salvage. Pushing aside his doubt and hesitation, he accepted the offer, resigned from Shaw Savill, and for a period found the change worthwhile. The depression, however, decided shipowners that the recovery of wrecked or damaged ships was not a good investment; indeed, the loss of a ship was often a relief. By January 1933 Aitchison was back again with Shaw Savill as chief officer.

It was plain sailing for him from now on . . . staff captain in the new *Dominion Monarch* in 1938 to September 1941 . . . master of *Empire Grace*, his first command, for five years . . . master of *Athenic, New Australia, Dominion Monarch, Gothic* . . . and now first master of *Southern Cross*.

Leadenhall Street gave him an experienced staff, with many of whom he had sailed before: Chief Officer, Angus Baber; First Officer, W. W. Newport; Chief Engineer, O. L. Jones; First Engineer, A. C. Ketley; Purser, R. D. Oliver; Catering Officer, S. L. Browne. They all arrived at Belfast before *Southern Cross* went on her trials, and were soon a well-knit team.

Baber, in fact, had been in Belfast with H. M. Rome, both of them from the Line's Marine Department, throughout the time *Southern Cross* was being built. They collaborated with Harland and Wolff, attended monthly meetings when Sanderson flew over with Lockhart and Craig, and also flew to London for consultations. They spent three months planning how passengers and crew would reach their muster-stations and lifeboats from their cabins in an emergency. There

was little they did not know about the ship, and the
job each man would have to do.

Equally knowledgeable was T. W. Watson, who co-
ordinated an immense amount of detailed work for the
ship in the management department at Leadenhall
Street. Watson had joined the Line in 1946 after service
in the Royal Navy as Lieutenant Commander R.N.V.R.
He was made an assistant manager in 1955; he is now
assistant manager for New Zealand in the Wellington
office.

As the date for the trials approached there was
animation in Leadenhall Street as well as in the ship.
As Craig told the Institute of Marine Engineers,
there were so many queries, for *Southern Cross* was
something different. Everyone wondered how all
would work out now that she was at long last to enter
her natural element, the open sea. All who had been
directly concerned during the long building period
had a sense of excitement as she moved under her own
power out of Belfast Lough and felt for the first time
in her life the surge of the sea.

"To everybody's surprise, there was no need for the
slightest worry," said Craig. "The ship behaved so
well, the absence of noise and vibration was so marked,
that it seemed too good to be true. Everything was not
perfect, but the faults were small and easily corrected.
Trim and condition of the ship were near enough to
what it would be in service on normal voyages."

The most contented man aboard was Sanderson.

His dream, his vision, his imagination had come
true. It was said of him that he knew the position of
every bolt in the ship. Throughout her building he
had flown many times to Belfast, courteous, alert,
probing, persistent, receptive, firm of decision, and
always ready with new ideas. One of these was the
Tavern, which was to become so popular.

Yet when *Southern Cross* sailed on her maiden voyage from Southampton on March 29th, 1955, there was still some justifiable reserve. Would she be liked by passengers; would she pay her way? She still had to prove herself.

She was given a tremendous and traditional send-off, and at every port along the route the scene was repeated. Sir David Aitchison had few worries—although he could have wished that the weather in the Atlantic might have been more placid during the first few days —and throughout the voyage Keville, the deputy chairman, was on board to check passenger-reaction and complaints, for no ship has yet sailed in which there has not been at least one complaining passenger.

After her return to Southampton there was no doubt that she would be popular, or that she could keep to her strict timetable. There was every reason to believe that she would be profitable.

A pause followed before *Southern Cross* made her second voyage. Sanderson decided to send her on three cruises in the Mediterranean and Atlantic during July and August. She was a full ship again when she next set out to circle the world.

And Sanderson already had plans—for a sister ship.

CHAPTER FIVE

A Year of Decisions

ON a June day in 1958, nearly six years after that July meeting when *Southern Cross* became a fact, if only on paper, Sanderson was at Ayot Bury waiting for a man whom he had summoned half across the world from Wellington, a man who—if everything went as he anticipated—would one day succeed him, first as managing director of Shaw Savill, and then as chairman, a man who was no doubt wondering why he had been sent for.

Sanderson had now been chairman for eleven years, and in that time the company's fleet had been rebuilt; no fewer than twenty-three new ships sailed the seas, and of the old pre-War and Wartime-built ships only seven remained. *Southern Cross* was a success. There was no doubt about it. On her first twelve voyages she had been 91 per cent full, a record no other passenger ship afloat could touch. The time was now approaching when all her experience, carefully noted and recorded, should be used in the building of a sister ship.

It had been quite clear, even before the Queen launched *Southern Cross*, that the Line was committing itself to two ships if it were going to provide a regular and sufficient service for the passengers who were wanting to travel. Two ships would mean that one could sail every six weeks from Southampton, and touch at ports along the route at the same interval; if one followed the eastbound route via Cape Town and the other the westbound via Panama, then passengers would be offered a number of alternatives. They could break their journey at any port on either of the routes, knowing they could go aboard again three months later; or they could wait at any port for the sister ship and return home covering the same stretch of sea as on their outward trip. There could be any number of permutations: Southampton to Las Palmas or Trinidad and back; Cape Town to Sydney or Wellington and back; Wellington to London and back. And so on.

Yet the outlay of further millions of pounds was not to be entered on lightly. Much had been learned. For instance, passengers soon sorted themselves out after a day or so at sea, with the more elderly settling into the forward lounge, the middle-aged preferring the smoke-room, and the high-spirited and the younger fry taking over the Tavern. But if there was joy and revelry by night in the Tavern, passengers seeking sleep in the cabins directly underneath could not be expected to be amused. In a sister ship there should be no cabins under the Tavern. The swimming-pool on the lower deck had been a partial success. Not only was there condensation, but, with a sea running and the stabilizers operating, the water in the pool had a habit of spouting geyserlike to the ceiling. One big pool on the sun deck would be more popular and less trouble.

These and many other points had been noted during the past three and a half years while planning for a sister ship had steadily taken shape. A number of decisions would be required. There was one, Sanderson knew, that he would have to take about his own position in the company.

He was now sixty-four, and retiring age for everybody in the Line was sixty-five. If things had worked

"The lettering 'Southern Cross' appeared on the stern" (p. 49)

Photos by courtesy of Harland and Wolff

"She was away to a burst of cheering and cacophony of hooters" (p. 51)

"John Collins presented the Queen with lilies of the valley" (p. 51)

"This was the moment for which Sanderson had planned." (*Left to right*)
Sir Frederick Rebbeck, Lord Wakehurst, the Queen, Basil Sanderson

out as planned a few years before, Keville would have succeeded him as chairman; but Keville had accepted an invitation to become deputy chairman of Furness Withy, the parent company, a position for which he was admirably suited. It was a good appointment, but it left Sanderson without a trained first lieutenant and a successor, who should be in from the start if a sister to *Southern Cross* were to be built.

As Sanderson paced the turf at Ayot Bury he told himself again that it would be unfair to expect any man to step abruptly into the chair without three or perhaps four years' grooming, especially if a new passenger liner were to be ordered. This meant that he would have to break the retiring-age rule and remain a little longer.

He had no doubt who his successor should be—the man for whom he was now waiting, John MacConochie, the Line's manager in New Zealand, protégé of his old friend John Macmillan, the bluff and generous-hearted Scot with whom he had first worked over thirty years ago.

Macmillan was dead now, but Sanderson would never forget him and the many things he had learned from him, particularly his promptness in taking decisions.

He remembered Macmillan often saying, "There are probably nine different ways of tackling a problem. Two are fatal—disastrous. Four are marginal. Three are good. If you take decisions quickly enough the marginals turn out right. The important thing is to act before anybody else. Move first, and you have the initiative. If you're wrong, well, that's bad luck."

Macmillan never wasted time drafting a letter with all the 'i's' dotted and the 't's' crossed. He would take a decision, send off a letter, and usually be in first. A polished version might follow at leisure.

Macmillan also gave Shaw Savill men full power to

5

act. "Why keep a dog and bark yourself?" he would say. Sometimes he barked at decisions taken, but in private. Always he supported his staff against outside criticism. Beneath his gruffness he had a warm heart. During the years of depression he had many visitors, and his raised voice was often heard behind his closed door; but the visitors rarely left without some kind of material comfort.

As a young man, fresh from Scotland, he had taken a liking to another Scot about his own age, William MacConochie, who had moved from the Border country to become a schoolteacher at Longtown, and later, with a wife from Manchester and a growing family, decided that accountancy in London offered a better future. The two Macs had met while Mac-Conochie was working on the accounts of the Bucknall Steamship Company, and had seen each other frequently to sink a dram or two and discuss the world and his wife; and on April 12th, 1908, to wet the head of John, MacConochie's sixth child.

Six years later Macmillan was at the graveside of his friend, whose life was cut short by pleurisy and whose widow now had the family to fend for; and while the raw soil was yet to cover the coffin Macmillan took on himself the responsibility of seeing that young John and his sister, Agnes, eighteen months older, were given a good schooling. He arranged for them to go to the Royal Caledonian School at Bushey, in Hertfordshire, an orphanage whose history went back to the aftermath of Waterloo, when it was started to educate the children of Scots killed during the Napoleonic wars.

When Agnes left school Macmillan engaged her as a telephonist in Shaw Savill, and he kept an eye on John when he started work over a year later as an office-boy with a firm of men's wholesale outfitters in

Wood Street, Cheapside. There John, bright, alert,
with deep-brown eyes, brown hair, a cleft chin, and an
easy, broad smile, swept floors, wrapped parcels,
and escorted Agnes to work from their home at Barnet.
But Agnes had little time to enjoy life. She died in
1927 from pneumonia.

Macmillan liked the letter he received from young
MacConochie thanking him for his sympathy, and
suggesting that a MacConochie should continue to
work for Shaw Savill. He offered the nineteen-year-old
boy a job as a junior in the freight department, and
advised him to take up shorthand and typing. For the
next three years MacConochie learned office routine
and delivered bills of lading to shipping companies
carrying cargo to Continental ports; he spent his
evenings at classes and worked up moderate speeds
at his two subjects.

Sanderson remembered Macmillan's pleasure at
finding his old friend's son as bright as a newly
minted penny, quick, cheerful, with an excellent
memory. He began to take an interest in MacConochie
himself, and watched his progress in the canvassing
department, where his personality was an asset. Often
he would suggest to Macmillan that the youngster
should be given some experience of ships.

"No need to move him," Macmillan would growl.
"He knows it all already."

In 1938 MacConochie married Peggy Martindale,
daughter of a music and mathematics master at St
Dunstan's College, Catford. He was now thirty, time
for him to settle down, Macmillan said.

At the Ministry of War Transport Sanderson kept
MacConochie in mind; being in a reserved occupation,
he had continued with Shaw Savill and also become a
special constable. When Sanderson began looking for
men for overseas posts he applied for MacConochie

to be seconded, and sent him out to Accra in 1942 to join the staff of Lord Swinton, Resident Minister for West Africa.

MacConochie sailed in *Henry Stanley*, in convoy. It was the first time he had been to sea, and it was a dull voyage. A watch was kept day and night for submarines, and the ship was blacked out at dusk. The alarm-bells rang three times, once when a porpoise was sighted. *Henry Stanley* was torpedoed on her next voyage.

By then MacConochie was comfortably settled in a hut with a thatched roof at Achimota College, a mile or so from Accra, where Lord Swinton had his headquarters. West Africa was now a vital link in the desert war in North Africa. The Mediterranean was closed to British shipping, Malta under siege, Rommel and his Afrika Corps surging on to El Alamein. Supplies for the Eighth Army, particularly aircraft, were urgent.

One way of getting aircraft to the desert war was to ship them in crates to Takoradi, which was under Lord Swinton's jurisdiction, unload them, assemble them, and have them flown across Northern Africa. A steady stream of some 500 aircraft a month arrived and were ferried to the desert by RAF pilots. MacConochie was appointed as the Ministry of Transport's representative for the Gold Coast, with headquarters at Takoradi, and supervised the shipping.

There were other valuable cargoes—stores for military and civilian needs in the four British Colonies, including the Gold Coast and Nigeria. There were also arrangements to be made for crews from the ships on shore leave, men who wanted some place in a foreign city where they would be among their own people. One answer was to provide clubs, where they could meet their mates and men of their own calling and drink good English beer. The selection and supervision of these clubs came under MacConochie's wing, and he was in no way disturbed when the British Sailors' Society was inclined to be concerned after it learned of the sale of beer and spirits in them. It was obvious to him that the crews would get their liquor somewhere, whatever the cost, and he preferred that they should obtain it in British clubs.

(He was to discover later that the Ministry of War Transport's decisions of this kind in West African ports were less complicated than those of its office in neutral Lisbon. There the crews had the enticement of brothels, thoughtfully backed by the Nazis, where loosened tongues might unthinkingly mention ships and the dates of their sailing and arriving. This gambit was countered by the British, who opened similar establishments, deciding that competition was preferable to a well-informed Gestapo. The profits from them were duly recorded and included in the accounts sent to Berkeley Square. The comments of the London Civil Servants on learning of this un-anticipated contribution to Government's revenue have not been recorded, not permanently at least.)

Eighteen months passed; the War moved on. In London plans were completed for Overlord, the invasion of Normandy. Once the Allied armies were ashore a shipping service would be needed to keep it supplied. The Ministry of War Transport were now looking for personnel. MacConochie was on its list, which meant his return to England.

There was a moment when his chances seemed slight. Before leaving for London the Ministry wanted him to visit Lagos, and he boarded *Phemius* in Takoradi for the reasonably short trip. He was shown to a bunk on a lower deck, and although he would have preferred a berth above the water-line, he settled down comfortably for the night. The ship was making an unescorted run, her captain hoping that speed would keep her clear of the U-boats, now hunting in packs.

MacConochie was asleep when two torpedoes struck. He woke to find himself floundering in fuel-oil, but with time to make a slippery way to the deck and with the consolation that he had gone to his bunk fully clothed and wearing his life-jacket. He was told to jump for it and make for a lifeboat. He jumped, and was nauseated as he swallowed fuel-oil with sea water. He was hauled into a lifeboat, where he was violently sick and not particularly interested when the U-boat surfaced alongside.

The conning-tower opened, sailors armed with rifles and fixed bayonets appeared, followed by the captain.

"Gentlemen," he said, "I shall require one of you to come aboard. Make your own selection. But be quick."

The radio officer from *Phemius* volunteered, clambered on to the submarine, and went into the conning-tower. By the time MacConochie had rid himself of the worst effects of the fuel-oil the submarine and the ship had gone. The remainder of the night was black and miserable, relieved only when he discovered a tin of cigarettes in a pocket, dry and palatable, and handed them round to his damp companions. They were sighted next day by a small French craft, and taken to Takoradi.

The visit to Lagos was abandoned, and his immediate problem was to arrange for the survivors of *Phemius* to return to England, and to get there himself. The quickest way, though not necessarily the safest, was to fly, and he returned home by air via Gibraltar. Peggy had no doubt that he had fully deserved the M.B.E. awarded for his work in West Africa.

At the Ministry in Berkeley Square teams were being formed to supervise the discharge of ships that would tie up alongside the Mulberry harbours on the invasion beaches. One team was to be attached to 21st Army Group headquarters, and MacConochie was among the first to arrive in a tank-landing craft and set up his camp-bed in a tent under the shelter of Normandy apple-trees a little way inland from Arromanches. The 'noises off' reminded him of the London blitz. But now the tide had turned, and shipping was still vital.

The ships arrived, the armies were kept supplied, the Wehrmacht was driven out of France, and 21st Army Group moved its headquarters to Louveciennes, near Paris, and there the Ministry team settled into a villa where the Gestapo had lately kept its Alsatians. The War was ending. Before it was over MacConochie was sent to Marseilles to direct the Ministry's work, and then on to Naples. The alliteration was the same— ships, supplies, stores, seamen. He returned to Shaw Savill in June 1946.

Sanderson made MacConochie an assistant manager, and found him invaluable throughout the phase of recovering the Shaw Savill fleet from naval service and re-equipping it. Three years later, in 1949, it was decided that MacConochie should look at the Line's operations on the other side of the world, and spend two years in Wellington, followed by two more in Sydney.

In November he sailed in *Athenic* with Peggy, Janet (aged seven), and Angus (eighteen months), and was assistant manager in Wellington until 1951, when he became manager in Sydney. He did so well that in 1953 he was asked to return to Wellington as manager. The following year he brought the family home in *Dominion Monarch* for the launching of *Southern Cross*. Back in Wellington, MacConochie was appointed a director of the Line in 1957. There was no doubt of his ability.

Now, in June 1958, the wheel of time was turning for Sanderson and for the Line, and decisions had to be taken: to single out his successor, and to build a new passenger ship to replace *Dominion Monarch* and dovetail it into service with *Southern Cross*. He had cabled MacConochie to fly from Wellington for a visit of about a week, and invited him to Ayot Bury when he had rested after the long flight. But, on landing at London Airport, MacConochie telephoned to say he was in no need of rest; he was coming straight on.

When he arrived the two men strolled round the garden and settled at length on a seat by the croquet lawn, and there Sanderson said he felt the time had come for MacConochie to leave Wellington and return to London. He mentioned Keville's appointment, and the planning for the new ship, but he gave no specific indication of the rungs on the ladder ahead of MacConochie, who guessed, no doubt, what they could be.

A fortnight or so later MacConochie was back in Wellington, and in November 1958 he and Peggy and Janet and Angus sailed in *Southern Cross* for Southampton; and early in the following year they settled into Red Gables, a large and roomy house at Hockering, on the outskirts of Woking, in Surrey, with a broad expanse of garden, well stocked with roses and flowering shrubs.

On June 19th, 1959, Sanderson handed over the work of managing director to MacConochie, and continued as chairman; and MacConochie reflected that it was just on thirty-two years since he had written to Macmillan, and that he now sat in the chair occupied then by his father's friend.

It was a year of decisions, and many of these were

concerned with the new ship. Suggestions for improvements, based on the experience of *Southern Cross*, were studied and debated by the Shaw Savill team, and it was agreed that, except on points of detail, no improvements in the design of the ship could be suggested. "This would seem to be unique," Sanderson observed.

It was decided, however, that she should be bigger than *Southern Cross*—24,733 tons compared with 20,400 tons; that she should be four feet wider, and fifty feet longer; that 1400 passengers should be carried instead of 1160; that there should be two alleyways up and down the ship, instead of one central alleyway, to save one foot six inches of width on every deck; that shaft horsepower be increased from 20,000 to 22,000; that there should be air-conditioning throughout—including the public lounges, with the exception of the Tavern, and also in the officers' quarters.

There would also be a number of other changes: the purser's office, the shops, and the hairdressing saloons should be under the Tavern and cabins midships as far as possible; the main swimming-pool would be transferred from the lower deck to the sun deck, and there would be pools for learners, non-swimmers, a paddling-pool for children, and a swimming-pool for the crew. There would be an observation deck on top of the bridge, eighty-seven feet above sea-level, which would give amateur photographers good views for their cameras and ciné-cameras. There would be special facilities for teenagers—a reception room with a juke-box and soft drinks. There would be relayed television, with sets at eleven points.

The shape of the funnel, the stern, and the bow and the central mast would also differ from those of *Southern Cross*. A wider range of plastics was now available and would replace wooden panelling in stairways. Cabins would be large, and wardrobes built on dividing walls to aid sound-proofing. There would be a bigger distillation plant, with a capacity of 500 tons a day instead of 300 tons; and the air-conditioning plant would provide another thirty tons a day in the tropics for the boilers. A launderette would be an improvement over the wash-troughs and drying-room in *Southern Cross*.

The ship would have a maximum speed of twenty-two knots, two instead of three boilers, and alternating electric current instead of direct current.

When all these and other decisions were taken tenders were invited. Sanderson anticipated that the Line would have to find around £7 million, but the shipbuilding industry was going through an indifferent period, and Vickers-Armstrongs (Shipbuilders) Ltd submitted the lowest tender and obtained the order. This was placed on December 9th, 1959, at a considerably lower figure than had been anticipated.

From now on there were consultations between the Shaw Savill team, including Lockhart and G. S. Jackson, who had succeeded Craig as engineering superintendent, and the Vickers-Armstrongs team, among them C. G. H. Houlden, managing director, R. J. W. Rudkin, director and manager of the Walker Naval Yard at Wallsend, and R. V. Turner, naval architect. And just as they had gone to Belfast, so Rome and Baber went to Walker-on-Tyne to stand by the new ship while she was being built.

On March 11th, 1960, the name of the new ship was published—*Northern Star*. The constellation known as the Plough, it was agreed, was an appropriate group to match the *Southern Cross*. Its 'pointers' enable even the most amateur astrologer to find the north star, which Shakespeare called "Northern Star" in Act 3, Scene 1 of *Julius Caesar*: "But I am constant as the northern star, of whose true-fix'd and resting quality there is no fellow in the firmament."

It was also decided that *Northern Star*'s keel would be laid in April (it was laid on the 29th), that she would be launched in June 1961, and begin her round-the-world service in "mid-1962".

There were several announcements in 1960.

One early morning in June Sanderson was awakened by a pounding on the front door at Ayot Bury, and in the moments while he was groping for his dressing-gown he wondered idly whether the house had been burgled. Downstairs he discovered that the nocturnal visitor brought very different news—confirmation of something he had known for several weeks, that he had been made a Baron by the Queen in the Birthday Honours List, and that the Lord Chamberlain was now sending him by express delivery a number of documents and a summons to take his seat in the House of Lords.

It was a recognition of his many services to the shipping industry, and the next few days brought a flood of congratulations from all over Britain and many parts of the world.

That same month it was announced that *Northern Star* would be launched on June 27th, 1961, and that her maiden voyage was fixed for mid-July the following year. Captain L. H. Edmeads, who had commanded *Southern Cross* since the retirement in 1957 of Sir David Aitchison, was to command the new ship, and Captain L. J. Hopkins, master of *Gothic*, would succeed him in *Southern Cross*.

Another item of news was published in the New Year which gave the Line abiding satisfaction: Queen Elizabeth the Queen Mother had consented to launch *Northern Star*.

During the following months MacConochie consulted the Queen Mother's secretary, Sir Martin Gilliat, from time to time over the arrangements, and when running over a list of suggested do's and don'ts a word of caution was included: please be careful to see that the bottle of wine for the naming ceremony does not become overheated. At one launching the bottle exploded, and there had been danger from splintering glass. MacConochie made a note that the bottle should be opened and the cork removed in good time.

When *Northern Star* was launched by the Queen Mother on June 27th the bottle of wine was, in fact, suspended from beneath the stem of the ship instead of the usual position high upon the bows. There was good reason for this change.

Shortly before, the Queen Mother had broken a bone in her left ankle and was obliged to cancel her engagements. One, however, she insisted on keeping— the launching of *Northern Star*. Since walking was out of the question, arrangements were made for her to be wheeled in a chair from a car to the launching-platform. This was reduced in height from twenty feet to eight feet, and a special ramp was built so that the chair could be wheeled up a gentle gradient.

The scene was similar to the launching of *Southern Cross* at Belfast—the great ship towering above, resplendent in her fresh grey and light-green paint, the assembled guests and workmen and their families, the sense of an occasion. The main difference was that the Queen Mother, who travelled north by train, brought fine weather with her—a sunny, gusty day which kept the flags and the bunting lively and gay. She was greeted by Viscount Knollys, chairman of Vickers Ltd, by Sir Charles Dunphie, chairman of Vickers-Armstrongs (Shipbuilders) Ltd, and by Lord Sanderson.

On the platform, she left the wheel-chair and, six minutes early, released the wine and the ship with the traditional: "I name this ship *Northern Star*. May God protect her and all who sail in her." Moments later *Northern Star* made her curtsy as she entered the Tyne.

A tribute to the Queen Mother's "typical courage and determination not to disappoint people by carrying through her programme today despite discomfiture from injury" was paid by Viscount Knollys at the function which followed. As a memento of the launching he presented her with a trinket-box and an unfinished portrait of her by Augustus John, R.A.

The Queen Mother recalled that she had sat for the portrait at Buckingham Palace, "but the sittings had to stop in 1940 when the War got bad." It was taken away from the Palace, but the sittings were never resumed because the War lasted so long. She also recalled that she had last been at the Walker Naval Yard twenty-two years before when her husband had launched the battleship *King George V*.

"A few months later," she continued, "our shipyards were at once in the forefront of the battle and our very survival depended on the valour and industry of those who toiled day and night to build and maintain the ships of our Royal and Merchant Navies.

"I would like to pay them my tribute today. Some, I know, are still working; others, perhaps, in retirement are watching the next generation uphold the fine tradition of the past. Changing times have brought new problems, and the shipbuilding industry today is faced with many difficulties.

"Of one thing I am certain—the creative genius of our nation flowers as brightly as ever, and British craftsmanship and skill cannot be rivalled anywhere in the world."

There were no better ambassadors than ships, she continued. They moved peaceably upon the great waters—the servants of commerce, the friends of all. And it was indeed fitting that a seafaring nation should, even in this age of air travel, continue to build fine ships which would, as of old, ply between the peace-loving countries of the world.

"The launching of a great ship is, I always think, a most moving occasion, but we must not regard this ceremony as an isolated event complete in itself. It is but one link in a massive chain of hard work, skill, and enterprise carried out by a host of people. Whether they play a large part or a small, all are partners in a great endeavour, and today all can take pride in this, their latest achievement, *Northern Star*."

Lord Sanderson said that *Northern Star* was born of confidence alone, "for in these days political events play havoc with estimates." Without confidence Britain's shipping industry could not survive.

The delivery of *Northern Star* would complete, for the time being, the Shaw Savill passenger-ship programme. She would join *Southern Cross* on their round-the-world service.

"Our company," he added, "can be relied upon to see that, in performance of their duties to the great travelling public, these two vessels live up to the prestige and high augury of the royal sponsorship which both have been so privileged to receive."

It was nearly a year later, on June 19th, 1962, that *Northern Star* left the Tyne to sail round Scotland for her trials on the measured course off the Isle of Arran.

The sequence of her completion was much the same as for *Southern Cross*. The engines—or machinery installation—was by Parsons Marine Turbine Company. Power to propel the twin screws, four-bladed and eighteen feet three inches in diameter, was to come from two independent sets of double-reduction

geared turbines designed by Pametrada and manu-
factured by Parsons. The machinery was designed for
a maximum of 22,000 steam horse-power for the two
shafts, with propeller revolutions of 120 a minute.
The astern turbines were to be capable of developing
60 per cent of the maximum ahead power. The main
boiler system was to consist of two Babcock and Wilcox
selectable superheat-type boilers designed for a pressure of 665 pounds per square inch at the steam
drum, with a controlled superheat temperature of
900° F.

As for *Southern Cross*, so there was for *Northern Star*
a series of tests in a wind-tunnel to make sure that
smoke and fumes would be ejected well clear of the
decks in a following wind, a point even more important
in *Northern Star* than *Southern Cross* since the lido
with its swimming-pools was placed immediately
in front of the funnel and would be a main centre of
ship life in fine weather. The behaviour of air-flow
over the decks and its effect on the comfort of
passengers was also studied.

While the ship was gradually being completed the
funnel was built of pre-fabricated aluminium; weighing
30 tons and 43 feet high, it was placed into position
by a 250-ton hammerhead crane eight months after
launching during a lull in a snowstorm on February
26th, 1962.

Throughout this time, too, and almost to the hour
when *Northern Star* set off down the Tyne—the last
passenger-ship to be built in Britain for some time—
the working of furnishing and decorating the cabins
and public rooms was proceeding.

Sanderson invited Miss Evelyn Pinching, an interior
decorator and a friend of Mrs Ainley's daughter,
Mrs Somervell, to act as consultant for the decorations
of the public rooms. It was the first time that Miss

Pinching had been associated with a ship, and, while she accepted the invitation a little tentatively, thinking that Sanderson was taking something of a risk, she was—as a former world champion and Olympic skier —used to taking risks herself.

By courtesy of Harland and Wolff

A lounge in *Southern Cross*: (*Above*) Taking shape; (*Below*) "It gave an
illusion of being circular" (p. 55)   80

By courtesy of Stuart Bale

By courtesy of Harland and Wo

Southern Cross on her trials: "his dream, his vision, his imagination had come true" (p. 61)

Northern Star—full steam ahead

By courtesy of Turners (Photography)

CHAPTER SIX

Design for Comfort

IT was November 1961 before Evelyn Pinching could begin work in *Northern Star*. She was determined that each public room should be given an atmosphere to suit its purpose. Once she had settled on fundamentals, and got what she described as "the bones" right, then she could go ahead with her planning.

She decided first to settle the shape of the deckheads, or ceilings, which in some cases were dominated by beams and awkward pieces of machinery, and to build the rooms to fit in with their main characteristics. Once the ceilings and the rooms were designed, seating and furniture could be adapted and colour schemes selected.

There were many problems. How would it be best, for instance, to provide sufficient seating and yet avoid the rooms looking as though they were cluttered up with furniture and chairs? The answer was small and light furniture and a certain amount of banquette seating—rather like a long sofa alongside a wall. What colours should be used? Normally colours in a room are influenced by its carpets. But carpets are expensive, and passengers have a habit of being forgetful with cigarette butts and drinks and coffee. This meant that in some cases the colour of the floors would be chosen first, in others the colours of the walls.

It meant days of planning, and planning at long range

in London at weekly meetings with the contractors until the ceilings and walls were completed in the ship's several rooms. Everything had to be visualized, and read correctly off the plans; and while this had a fascination, Miss Pinching sometimes found it hard on the nerves. It was a little easier once the walls and ceilings were completed and there was purpose in monthly visits to the ship to see how the work was progressing; but often it seemed that the rooms would not be ready before the ship sailed from the Tyne, and it was not until she went aboard for the trip round Scotland, bound for the trials off the Isle of Arran, that she saw the result of nearly two years' work for the first time.

Several problems arose in the forward lounge. One was caused by the sheer, or sharp rise, in the deck which almost gave the impression of walking uphill. This was evened out by building a raised platform at the far end of the room nearest the ship's bows. Then there were four large pillars which were not central, but which, once the platform was in position, became the centre area and allowed the arrangement of groups of furniture to break up the expanse of the room.

The colour of the walls was chosen first mainly because the several loudspeakers needed to be hidden and covered by a material which would not interfere with sound. An attractive terracotta was selected, and it was decided to use it to cover both loudspeakers and the walls. It looked better on a black rather than a white background, but there were several puzzled faces for a time when all the walls were jet black, before the terracotta was put on. To relieve this rather dark background, pale yellow and brown silk curtains were hung, and these colours were repeated in the furniture coverings; a neutral colour was used for the floor. Attractive prints of balloons were bought at

Sotheby's to enliven the walls. Two large china vases from the *Dominion Monarch* were placed in alcoves.

There were few problems about the smoke-room, almost in the centre of the ship. The ceilings gave no trouble, there was no sheer, three bays in each of the outer walls lent some character. Banquette seating was repeated in them, and acid yellow used as a covering and for the curtains, which at night gave an illusion of height. Card-tables with reversible tops, laminated one side with green baize on the other, were kept in the centre of the room, and a number of coffee-tables had a design from a Maori carving.

The walls were panelled in aspen veneer with rosewood pillars as a contrast, and to fill blank spaces drawings of sea-birds in fibre-glass were placed on the forward walls. Later, three paintings of sea-birds by Robin Hall, of Melbourne, were hung.

Another feature was a pendulum clock showing Greenwich Mean time, and also the time in twelve cities—Calcutta, Cape Town, Colombo, Delhi, Dublin, Edinburgh, Kingston (Jamaica), Melbourne, Ottawa, Shanghai, Sierre Leone, and Wellington. Miss Pinching found it in the Portobello Road, in London, and although she disliked its Victorian case—it was about 130 years old—she thought it was just the thing for the smoke-lounge. The pendulum was replaced by electricity, and the clocks were removed from the case and built into the panelling of the wall.

The cinema presented a number of conundrums. It was the largest of the public rooms, and it had to be multi-purpose—a lounge by day and either a cinema or a ballroom by night. Account had to be taken of the stage and cinema screen, and also of the balcony extending out into the room, giving part of it an area of low ceiling and an atmosphere of darkness.

These two features formed an ellipse, and this

became the motif, into which the bay windows on either side of the ship were worked. The dark area under the balcony was given an illuminated bar with a shuttered front. By day this front resembled a decorated wall, and at night the bar-lights blazed. The high ceiling was relieved by simulating the Great Bear and Little Bear focusing on the North Star.

The space for the Tavern was complicated, since it was shaped like an H, the upper half of the letter having to provide room for the funnel and swimming-pool. The bottom half was given the largest bar afloat—68 feet long; a dance-floor was arranged on one side, and tables and seats, divided into compartments or stalls, on the other. Timber was used for decoration, with a beamed ceiling over the bar and slatted Douglas fir for the remainder of the ceiling area. Bright-red panels behind the bar and bright-green panels facing it gave a splash of colour, and brackets in the shape of upside-down brandy glasses provided a novel form of lighting. Plaques of old English inns were presented by Whitbreads and placed on the various stalls. (They were rapidly acquired by souvenir-hunters. A fresh set had to be screwed in.) Seating in the windows was built low to give a good view of the sea from any position, and wide doors provided for dancing couples to twist on the open deck which runs almost to the ship's stern.

Bright colours were used to counter the effect of low ceilings in the two restaurants. The forward restaurant was given a green floor with green pillars and apricot-coloured chairs and banquette seating; the aft restaurant had these colours reversed—an apricot floor and pillars, and green chairs and banquette seating. Walnut plastic was used for the walls, ceilings, and dumb-waiters. There were sketches of Australian

animals round the walls, and the glass panels in the entrance doors, etched with Australian, New Zealand, and South African animals, came from *Dominion Monarch*.

After the big public rooms everything was fairly straightforward in the writing-room and library. The writing-room ceiling needed to be altered slightly to balance a row of windows; and, to avoid the appearance of desks and a classroom look, a central ring was formed; other desks were placed round the walls. The motif was blue and green with curtains repeating the colours on a white background. A touch of inspiration was the hanging of paintings by the Australian aborigines Albert Namatjira and Herbert Raberaba, which blended exceptionally well with the room.

In the library contrasts with the book-covers were the choice of a light carpet, dark furniture wood, and a black writing-desk of Regency design with touches of brass to give it light. Green hide was used for the chairs. An altar recess, for Communion services, was masked by a painting by Peter McIntyre, the New Zealand artist, of a panorama of Wellington.

Much thought was directed to the main entrance-hall, the passengers' introduction to the ship, and there the lowness of the ceiling was counteracted by lighting. Felix Kelly, the Auckland artist, who has lived in London since the 'thirties, was commissioned to provide two large murals. They were imaginary scenes, incorporating Shaw Savill ships against backgrounds of Table Mountain, Sydney Harbour, and Milford Sound. Under them were two Regency sofas; the colour Kelly selected for them was purple, which blended well with both the murals and the grey walls. The two entrances from the main hall to the forward lounge were darkened purposely to heighten the impact of brightness when entering the lounge.

There were no worries over the rooms for the teenagers and the infants' nursery. Mirrors were used to give a sense of space round the purser's office, the shop, and the hairdressing saloons.

Gradually the ship acquired character, and Evelyn Pinching was impatient to see the final result when she took the train north to board *Northern Star* to sail down the Tyne and round Scotland. She had mixed feelings; after two years' work she felt as though she were about to lose a part of her life.

Nobody imagined, when they went aboard, that a near disaster lay ahead of *Northern Star* at the mouth of the Tyne.

CHAPTER SEVEN

An Anxious Few Minutes

A STRONG, gusty north-east wind was blowing when *Northern Star* moved away from her berth at Walker-on-Tyne shortly after two o'clock on the afternoon of June 19th, 1962, and four tugs—two forward and two aft—took up their positions to shepherd her down the Tyne to the open sea. Dressed over-all, she was a splendid sight; and high on her mast the Vickers-Armstrongs House Flag flapped and quivered, and would continue to fly there until the trials were ended and she was formally accepted by Shaw Savill. The shipbuilders' senior master, Captain Blackwood, was in command, and with him on the bridge was the chief Tyne pilot, Captain Claude Ramsay.

Northern Star was a fortnight behind schedule, the result of a demand for more pay and a ban on overtime by the workmen completing the final touches. Tyneside was proud of her, yet sad to see her leave. Nearly eight thousand people—workmen, their wives and families, and the staffs of sub-contractors—had been aboard to see over her. Now work stopped in every yard, and thousands waved as she moved along, slowly and majestically, the river echoing to the tooting and shrilling of every hooter and whistle with sufficient steam to raise even the most emasculated peep.

It was an occasion, this farewell to Tyneside, and on board were the men of Vickers-Armstrongs who had

watched her grow from a keel plate—Houlden, and
Turner and Young, the naval architects, and others—
and from Shaw Savill Lord Sanderson and W. R.
Russell, the general manager, and those who had
planned and worked for her; and, of course, Captain
Edmeads, his officers and crew, who were impatient
to have the trials over and to be off on the maiden
voyage.

Edmeads was on the bridge, and with him was his
staff captain, Baber, glad that the long period of
standing by the new ship was ended, keen to be away
to sea again.

Edmeads, stocky, reserved, inclined to be shy,
regarded the passing Tyneside thoughtfully. He had
been at sea now for nearly forty-one years, and
Northern Star was his fifth command. He had seen
many changes since, a lad of nearly seventeen, he had
left his parents and his home at Gravesend, where he
was born and educated, and despite the disapproval of
his father—one of the Orient Line's shore staff—
started his merchant naval career with the Ellerman
Hall Line as a cadet. That was in 1921. Four years
later he had his second mate's ticket, and ten years
later his extra master's certificate.

He was glad to have it, but it didn't seem to help him
much during the start of the 'thirties, when he and
others found themselves ashore on reduced pay for
six months in every eighteen, and everybody complained
about the depression. Edmeads did more than complain. He applied to a number of companies for a job,
and in January 1934 he dropped down a couple of
notches and joined Shaw Savill as a fourth officer and
went aboard *Tamaroa*. By the outbreak of War he
was a second officer again. At the end of 1941 he
went to *Arawa* and stayed with her for eight years,
rising to chief officer. In June 1950 he was given his

first command, and in November 1957 he succeeded
Sir David Aitchison in *Southern Cross*. He had enjoyed
his four years in the Line's newest ship, particularly
running her to a time-schedule and not having to
worry about delays and hanging around ports for
cargo.

One of the many things he liked about ships and the
sea was that a man never stopped learning. There had
been plenty to learn about *Southern Cross*, for not only
was every ship different, but she was—well, more
different than others, seeing that she carried no cargo.
It meant among other things that there were no
worries about varying draughts, which, in a cargo-
ship, could change as much as twelve to fifteen feet
according to the state of its loading. *Southern Cross*
did not vary more than a couple of feet throughout a
voyage. Yet you had to keep an eye on her—in a strong
wind.

Southern Cross was undoubtedly 'wind-conscious'
with her massive superstructure; some people had the
idea that her funnel aft acted like a sail. Edmeads was
not particularly interested in this theory, but he knew
that while she handled like a yacht in calm, windless
weather, you had to watch her like a hawk in wind—
especially at slow speeds. She would turn broadside on
to a wind of any force if she was moving slowly.
This was a point Sir David had impressed on him—
and Sir David had found her a handful in the Mersey
one night in August 1957.

Southern Cross had landed her passengers in Liverpool and anchored in the Mersey before sailing for
Belfast and a refit the following day. Life was relaxed
until a north-west gale began and a strong ebb tide
started to run. With the combination of wind on her
superstructure and the tide, she began to drag her
anchors early in the morning, and for four hours the

engines were going ahead to keep her in the stream. At 8 A.M. Sir David put out to sea and sent a signal to Leadenhall Street reporting his change of position. He had not been unhappy at being told to proceed to Belfast.

As Edmeads refilled his cigarette-holder and glanced around at the overcast sky and noticed the straining bunting he wondered how *Northern Star* would handle in a high wind. He noticed, too, and Baber confirmed this, that she was trimmed three feet by the bow—that is to say, her bow was three feet deeper in the water than her stern. They had always found that *Southern Star* handled better if she were trimmed one foot by the stern—a difference of four feet. Edmeads could only reflect that he was an onlooker, that he might learn something about *Northern Star*, and if and how she differed in her handling from *Southern Cross*. But he could see that Baber was uneasy.

He was glad to have Baber with him to start the new ship on her service. They had been together in *Southern Cross*, and Baber—burly, thick-set, with his sideburns giving him a John Bull look—was a good man to have around.

Baber was a Scot with an English upbringing. He was born at Bridge of Allan, in Stirlingshire, and educated at Chipping Camden and Cinderford Grammar School, in Gloucestershire, where his father became a dairy-farmer after the First World War. Young Baber was more interested in the sea than the land, and he wanted to join the Royal Navy. When he was fifteen he went to H.M.S. *Worcester*, the Thames Nautical Training College, for three years; when the Second World War began he was Midshipman Baber, R.N.R., in the battleship *King George V*. He was in her when she took part in the sinking of the *Bismarck*. By the end of the War he was a lieutenant, and he would have been content to remain in the Royal Navy; he was not, however, interested in a temporary commission. He joined Shaw Savill, and sailed in *Mataroa* in July 1946 as fifth officer. In October 1953 he left *Athenic* to stand by *Southern Cross* with Rome, and he sailed in her for four years, from March 1955 until February 1959, when he had come up to Walker-on-Tyne for the building of *Northern Star*.

An hour and a half went by as *Northern Star* with her escort of puffing tugs moved sedately down the Tyne. Edmeads noted that young Reid, the first officer, who had not even been born when he had first gone to sea, was on the fo'c'sle with the carpenter, Alex Meikle, another Scot, handy to the anchors.

Reid, oval-faced, tubby, with an easy smile, was enjoying a pleasant feeling of mild excitement. Just on thirty, he had been with the Line for nearly thirteen years, and he had been standing by *Northern Star* since her launching, the first time he had watched a ship taking final shape. He felt exhilarated to be going to sea in a new ship, but he shared with Baber an uneasiness about *Northern Star* being trimmed by the bows, for he had also sailed in *Southern Cross*.

Reid had a feeling for ships, which was not altogether strange, for his father had been a master mariner and a second officer until he had married and set up in a florist's shop in Southampton. He had three uncles and a cousin at sea, and during the War his father served in the R.N.R. in sea transport.

At the end of 1949 Reid completed a course at the Southampton Navigation School, and was in *Athenic* as a cadet under Sir David Aitchison. By 1953 he had his second mate's certificate, and was in *Gothic* as fifth officer for the Royal Tour of New Zealand and Australia. Life at sea was all he hoped it would be. He was sorry when the tour ended at Aden, and he sensed that the Queen looked sad when she left to go aboard the royal yacht *Britannia*. He told his parents that it seemed she had almost regarded Sir David as "a sort of uncle".

After *Gothic*, Reid returned to *Dominion Monarch*, and he was third officer with his mate's certificate when he joined *Southern Cross* for her third voyage. By 1959 he was promoted, with his master's certificate, to *Ceramic*, and he had come on from her to *Northern Star*. He was married now, and his young wife had said she was going down to the breakwater at the mouth of the Tyne to watch the ship sail out into the North Sea. He might get a glimpse of her.

As the ship moved into the entrance to the river, formed by two breakwaters in the shape of a rough V, he felt chilly when the wind began to gust strongly. But he soon became busy after the two forward tugs cast off and he watched Captain Ramsay, the pilot, leave the ship. Everything seemed normal, and it would not be long now before they were clear of the river and he could leave the fo'c'sle.

As he looked over towards the south breakwater Reid wondered idly if his wife was among the small crowd; at the same time he noticed that *Northern Star*, moving slowly and with little way while the tugs were churning away from her, was heading to starboard towards the breakwater. He decided that it was to allow for leeway.

Suddenly he realized that *Northern Star* was turning into the wind, and that the breakwater was coming closer at a fair speed. A second or two later his telephone rang. It was Baber, on the bridge.

"Stand by your anchors," said the crisp Royal Naval accent.

"Aye, aye, sir," said Reid, and in the same breath shouted to Meikle, "Stand by anchors, Chippy."

"Aye, aye, sir."

A quick look at the breakwater, some fifty yards away, and Reid could see the small crowd beginning to scatter.

Again the telephone and Baber.

"Let go your port anchor."

Reid shouted the order, and Meikle's "Aye, aye, sir" was lost in the rattle of metal.

"Let go your starboard anchor."

Leaning over the ship and looking towards the stern, Reid could see the propellers churning—hard astern—and the tugs wheeling and making back towards *Northern Star*, their bows pushing walls of creaming sea.

Ten minutes or so later Edmeads was thoughtful. The tugs had been unable to swing *Northern Star* round to face the North Sea, and she was leaving the Tyne stern first. But they held her securely, and she had plenty of way on. There was no danger now, but it had been an anxious few minutes when the wind caught her. There had been tension and a quietness on the bridge you could feel while orders had been given sharply, and several expressionless faces masked a variety of feelings. Another minute or two and *Northern Star* would have ended up on the breakwater.

There, at least, one person had been unworried—Mrs Reid. When her companion said, "I wonder why they're dropping the anchors. Is anything wrong?" she replied, "Oh, no. It's just an exercise"—an observation that was later to cause her husband a fit of coughing which somehow seemed to suggest he was on the point of choking.

As *Northern Star* left the Tyne and felt the lift of the sea she dipped a curtsy, much as she had when the Queen Mother launched her; but there were some on board who felt her behaviour had been somewhat unladylike. The tugs took her a mile clear of the Tyne and tooted with relief as they bounced their way home. As she headed north for the run round Scotland her trim was altered so that she was slightly down by the stern.

After the trials off the Isle of Arran the ship was handed over officially by Richard Rudkin, yard manager to Vickers-Armstrongs, to Lockhart, who signed for her. The builders' House Flag was run down and the Shaw Savill Flag hoisted for the first time, and from that moment the Line became responsible for all costs ranging from the ship's insurance to the payment of the crew. MacConochie presented Rudkin with a silver jug for the builders' boardroom table—a token of appreciation and also an acknowledgment of their gift of a radiogram to the master and chief engineer—and, with his wife, looked forward to sailing in *Northern Star* on her maiden voyage as far as Cape Town.

Fortunately he did not know that if she had not behaved quite like a lady while leaving the Tyne she was going to become far more troublesome during the weeks ahead.

CHAPTER EIGHT

Chemical Action

JUST on four weeks after *Northern Star* left the Tyne she was nosing her way through a placid sea towards the tropics. On the bridge Reid felt relaxed and at home. Idly he watched the bows nodding gently at the straight line of the horizon, glanced at the passengers getting the last of the afternoon sun on the broad expanse of deck in front of the bridge—it was nearly half-past five and some would be off soon to the first dinner sitting—and enjoyed the contrast of the Air Force blue of the sky with the Navy blue of the Atlantic. It was a peaceful scene, and life aboard was settling into a routine, with Las Palmas two and Southampton six days behind.

Southampton and England seemed another world. It was almost a week, but it might as easily have been a month, since *Northern Star* left on her maiden voyage on July 10th and over 1400 passengers had come aboard and the rails on every deck had been crowded for a stirring send-off. Many of the 480-odd crew to whom the *Star* was another ship, another job, responded to the atmosphere.

It was still a little too soon to judge feelings and reactions in the ship and how the staff was coping with such a large number of people—250 more passengers than in *Southern Cross*.

Some of the officers were old shipmates, and Reid remembered Brew, the chief engineer—often referred to as "Daddy" Brew—from *Dominion Monarch* days. He had been Chief in the *Monarch* for ten years, and while standing by *Northern Star* when she was building he had done one voyage in the *Southern Cross* as supernumerary Chief to get experience of a ship with engines aft. Although he had been away from Maryport, in the Solway Firth, for most of his sixty years, Brew had not lost his Cumberland accent or his direct bluntness, which seemed to match his Punch-like features and his straight white hair.

A double ring on the starboard-engine telegraph startled Reid.

"What the . . .?" he thought. An emergency ring with the ship cruising at eighteen and a half knots could only mean trouble.

"Starboard engine stopped, sir," said the helmsman as Reid moved quickly towards the telegraph.

"Stopped?" he echoed.

"Aye, aye, sir."

Automatically, he checked the indicator, and the next moment was telephoning the captain.

At the same moment Brew was lifting his receiver in his cabin. He swore softly at the reply to his grunted "Yes?"

"Starboard engine's been stopped, sir," said a voice in the engine-room. "Sparks were coming from the h.p. turbine thruster plate. Oil temperature's gone up twenty degrees to one three four."

"I'll come away down," said Brew.

He had been about to change from his white boiler-suit, grubby with oil-stains, but now he grabbed his cap and thick, heavy gloves and stumped along the narrow corridor from his cabin to the port alleyway. A few moments later the stuffy heat of the engine-room and the deep grumble of machinery enveloped him as he clumped down the steel gangways into the depths of the ship.

"Trouble," he was thinking. "Well, that's what we're paid for."

He found a group of boiler-suited men round the starboard high-pressure turbine, among them Jack Worden, first engineer, and the men from Parsons Marine Turbine Company, and Pametrada, the engine-builders.

"Rotor indicator moved over against the rotor," Worden said, pitching his voice above the pulsing of the port engine. "Looks like the thrust bearing has packed up."

"We'd better open it up, find out why," said Brew.

"Looks as though the rotor has moved forward," said another engineer. "Something's shifted anyway."

"Well, get the lads on to it," said Brew.

His staff was twenty-eight officers, four cadets, and twenty ratings, all of whom had their set jobs during the watches. In addition to the main engine-room, the ship's electricity, refrigeration, air-conditioning, the galley and deck machinery, and the cinemas came under his wing. They all had a full day's work. If the thrust bearing had packed up—well, they really had trouble on their hands.

"I'll let the captain know," said Brew, and left the group to telephone Edmeads.

"Could be an hour or more before we find out what's happened," he told the captain.

Edmeads sent word to MacConochie, who came on to the bridge.

"Well, we can only wait," MacConochie said. Teething troubles were to be expected on a maiden voyage.

It was seven o'clock, and the gong had just rung for the second dinner sitting, before the next report came from the engine-room.

It was serious. Engineers, sweating in a temperature

7

around 95° F. found that the pads of the thrust
bearing had been completely worn away. Steel had
then rubbed against steel, and the thrust collar on the
turbine rotor had been badly corded. The rotor
had shifted nearly a quarter of an inch out of
position.

It meant that the high-pressure turbine on the
starboard engine was completely useless. It could not
be run again until fresh metal-lined thrust pads were
fitted, and the thrust collar machined true. This work
could not be done in the ship.

"We can still use the starboard engine?" Mac-
Conochie asked.

"We can get it going by cutting out the high-
pressure turbine and working the engine with the
low-pressure turbine only," he was told. "But it's
going to be a long and difficult job."

"How long?"

"Several hours."

"Tell me, roughly what has to be done."

"Well—remember that each engine has a high-
pressure and a low-pressure turbine. Both have a
thrust, which is on a shaft connecting the turbine
in the gearing. The turbines drive the gearing, which
in turn drives the propeller shaft."

"Yes."

"Steam from the boilers goes into the high-pressure
turbine. After various stages it then enters the low-
pressure turbine at a reduced pressure. Then it goes
on to the condenser, becomes water again, and is
pumped back into the boilers."

"Yes."

"As we can't use the starboard high-pressure
turbine, the steam will have to by-pass it and go
straight to the low-pressure turbine. Once we've
got the high-pressure turbine sealed off and the

low-pressure turbine going again we can start up the starboard engine."

"A big job."

"Pretty big."

In the engine-room, sweat-rags round their foreheads, their faces red and glistening, the engineers had begun dismantling the steam pipes connecting the two starboard turbines. All watches were reorganized with a skeleton staff to keep the remainder of the machinery running smoothly, and thirty men were packed in the confined space round the turbines.

"It's a shambles," Brew said.

Some men were disconnecting the high-pressure turbine from the gearing, others blanking off the oil-supply. Others were ripping away the lagging from the flanges where the pipes fitted on to the turbine casing.

There were bursts of graphic swearing when it was discovered that the nuts on the bolts in the overhead steam-pipe flanges could not be moved. One or two spanners burst, and hammers had no effect. Chisels were called for to cut the nuts away.

It was hell working just under the deckhead. There was little room to move to get a good bash with a hammer. The heat was around 160° F. The engineers could stay there for a couple of minutes only, and then, gasping and streaming sweat, they had to rest.

The work went on for twenty-five hours. Gradually emergency piping linked the boilers to the low-pressure turbine. And then, just after the second dinner sitting on July 17th, the starboard engine started again, and *Northern Star* began to pick up speed, creeping to eighteen and a half knots from fifteen.

During the next two days there were discussions by Brew and his engineers and the men from Parsons and Pametrada and MacConochie. Why had the white metal on the thrust pads worn away? There was nothing

wrong with the oiling system. Wireless messages went
off to Leadenhall Street, and were sent on to the
engine-makers. Engineers were booked to fly to
Cape Town.

"Keep an eye on the oil temperature on the port
h.p. turbine," Brew told Worden.

They were an interesting contrast of the older and
the younger engineers at sea—Brew, tall, burly, grey,
walking with a limp, the result of a fall in an oil-tanker
during the twenties; Worden, short, dark, with an
engine-room pallor, in his early thirties.

Both had served their apprenticeship in railway
workshops—Brew for five years in Maryport, from the
time he was sixteen, and Worden, the son of a black-
smith, at Lytham St Anne's shipyard. Worden had
learned his profession with the old London, Midland,
and Scottish Railway, which used to run small ships
of around 1000 tons from Fleetwood, near Blackpool,
to Ireland.

Brew, like so many of his generation, found the
outlook dour when his apprenticeship was completed
in 1923. He was twenty-one, but there seemed to be
no future in shipping, and he was determined to go to
sea. He did go to sea—to Canada, but in Montreal he
discovered that life was just as difficult as in Maryport.
The Bell Telephone Company employed him installing
telephones and then working on main telephone
exchanges. But this wasn't getting him to sea. He
joined the Canada Steamship Line which ran ships
on the Great Lakes, and found himself at a desk as a
superintendent's assistant. The job packed up in 1925
after a couple of years when the depression hit Canada.
He decided to return home. His cash was limited, but
he got himself a job in an American cattle-ship taking
850 cattle from St John, New Brunswick, to the
abattoirs in Birkenhead.

Things looked better in 1926. He joined Shaw Savill and went to sea in *Mahana* as a second refrigerator-watcher, working twelve hours on and twelve off. Two years later he was on the way up, sixth engineer in *Tainui*, with the memory of the year before when the *Mamari* struck an iceberg on the way round Cape Horn and shipped eighty tons of ice on the foredeck.

The 'thirties brought him steady promotion, and at the end of 1937 he was standing by as staff chief in Sunderland while the engines for *Dominion Monarch* were being built. He was in her for the maiden voyage, and stayed until 1941, when he went as chief engineer to *Empire Grace* before she was renamed *Wairangi*, and remained with her for six years. After the War he was chief engineer in *New Australia*, the immigrant ship, for two and a half years before returning to *Dominion Monarch* for ten years.

Life had not been so complicated for Worden when he finished his seven-year apprenticeship in 1950. He joined Shaw Savill as a junior engineer in May, and was amazed by the size of *Delphic*'s engines after those in the small ships running to Ireland. He got to know Auckland well when *Delphic* was delayed there for weeks during a waterside strike.

Worden found the next ten years varied and interesting and promotion regular . . . from *Delphic* to the old coal-burner, *Mahia* . . . to *Persic*, and turbines . . . to *Gothic*, and then to *Southern Cross* as second engineer in September 1957, followed by eight voyages in her as first engineer. A year ashore as staff engineer, relieving, and then he went to Walker-on-Tyne in January of 1962 to stand by *Northern Star*.

Like Brew, he accepted that trouble was a by-word in an engineer's life, but he hoped the *Star*'s engines were not going to play up any more on this trip.

During the next two days the engine-room was tidied while the *Star* churned on towards Cape Town, where the rotor would be lifted from the h.p. turbine and made ready for crating. When the ship reached Fremantle the crate would be flown to Cockatoo Island, in Sydney, and the thrust pads repaired. The rotor would be put back either there or in Melbourne, and the h.p. turbine reconnected.

Brew ordered a more frequent check on the oil temperatures of both starboard and port turbines. He was not altogether surprised when his telephone rang in the early hours of the morning of July 20th.

"Yes?" he inquired, blinking as he switched on his bedside light.

"Oil temperature on the port h.p. turbine thrust up five degrees, sir."

"Over what period?"

"The last quarter of an hour, sir."

"Humph. Well, you'd better reduce power. I'll be away down."

Brew replaced the receiver, sighed, swore, yawned, and got up. He was soon in his boiler-suit, capped and gloved. He started to sweat in the familiar heat as he went down the ladders in the engine-room.

"Oil temperature up another five degrees, sir," he was told when he reached the port h.p. turbine.

"Looks as though it could be the same trouble as on the starboard h.p."

"Could be, sir."

"Aye, it could be. Well, we'd better check. Have the port engine stopped. The lads will have to get to work again."

A few moments later Reid was telephoning from the bridge to Edmeads, asleep in his cabin.

"The engineers have stopped the port engine, sir," said Reid.

Edmeads glanced at his watch. It was just after three o'clock.

"I'll come up," he said. "I think you'd better inform Mr MacConochie."

"Aye, aye, sir."

Ten minutes later MacConochie and Edmeads were in the captain's sitting-room listening to the report of the superintendent engineer.

"We suspect it's the same trouble as in the starboard h.p. turbine," he said. "If it is we may not have enough spares to switch to the port l.p. turbine."

During the next two and a half hours MacConochie and Edmeads drank several cups of tea and smoked innumerable cigarettes. Gloomily they speculated on the cause of the trouble and the extent of the now inevitable disruption of *Northern Star*'s schedule. It was the worst of misfortune on her maiden voyage. At half-past five the superintendent engineer returned with the confirmation that the thrust pads of the turbine were almost as badly worn as those in the starboard h.p. turbine. The same operation would have to be repeated—the port h.p. turbine by-passed and emergency steam piping linked directly to the port l.p. turbine. Fortunately, there were sufficient spares. Until Melbourne at least, and possibly Sydney, *Northern Star* would be driven by two half-engines.

"What speed shall we have?" MacConochie asked.

"About sixteen knots," said the superintendent engineer.

"We shall be at least a day late at Cape Town," said Edmeads. "After that . . ."

All that day the engineers toiled again, working in two-hour shifts, ripping away lagging, blanking off oil and steam, bashing at seized bolts, and connecting emergency piping. Brew was proud of his men, particularly the four cadets. "They pigged in like little heroes. They would not miss any of it. They became engineers overnight," he said later. With the unwanted experience from the starboard h.p. turbine the engineers cut seven hours off their previous time, and had the port engine working again in eighteen hours.

A broadcast announcement was made to the passengers, and with the news that the ship would be behind schedule another section in *Northern Star* became busy—the radio room.

There, close to the bridge, the Chief Radio Officer, C. L. Carpenter, and his four radio officers had sent off messages about the turbines to Leadenhall Street as part of their routine. Whatever was happening in the engine-room, their job was to send and receive messages, tape-record news broadcasts and relay extracts to the cinema lounge each afternoon, bring out the daily news-sheet, put on television shows, relay concerts and dance music. Now they had to handle a flow of messages from passengers altering their private arrangements because of *Northern Star*'s changed schedule.

Carpenter, a West Countryman, tall, with thinning hair and a sandy moustache, quiet-spoken, and his young officers took it all in their stride. They were all Marconi-trained and employed and posted in *Northern Star* by Marconi, who had installed all the radio equipment. Now fifty-nine, Carpenter had trained at Bristol College and first gone to sea as a radio officer in 1921.

In December 1939 he was in *Trelissick*, which was bombed and sunk by a Heinkel in the North Sea. When Carpenter and others of the crew were safely aboard the destroyer *Pytchley* she struck a mine, and they were lucky to be picked up a second time.

There was a period when he felt it would be a case

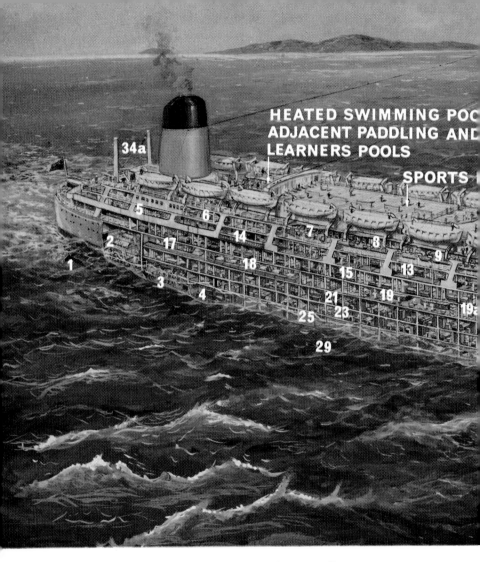

HEATED SWIMMING POO
ADJACENT PADDLING AND
LEARNERS POOLS

SPORTS

"Splendid Sisters"—*Northern Star* (in foreground)

Key to Numbers

1. Starboard propeller
2. Boiler Rooms
3. Starboard Steam Turbine Engine Room
4. Auxiliary Machinery Rooms
5. Recreation Rooms (starboard) and Infants' Playroom and Pool (Port)
6. Tavern
7. Cinema Lounge

8. Edge of Sun Deck (cut away)
9. Smoke Room
10. Entrances to Lifts and Stairs
11. Library
12. Forward Lounge
13. Cabins
14. Stowed Accommodation Ladder
15. Cabins

31
30
**HOUSETOP OBSERVATION
DECK**
32
33
SUN DECK
34
11
12
LOUNGE DECK
PROMENADE DECK
20
MAIN DECK
22 **RESTAURANT DECK**
24
22a **'A' DECK**
28 27
LOWER DECK
'B' DECK

Diagramatic drawing by G. H. Davis, S.M.A.

and *Southern Cross* (in background)

16.	Stairs and Lifts	26.	Store-rooms
17.	Cabins	27.	Baggage Rooms
18.	After Restaurant	28.	Fuel Tanks, etc.
19, 19a.	Galley and Pantries	29.	Starboard Stabiliser (stowed)
20.	Forward Restaurant	30.	Mast
21.	Cabins	31.	Crow's Nest with Secomak Whistle and Radar Scanner
22, 22a.	Crew Accommodation	32.	"Christmas Tree" signal-light post
23.	Cabins		
24.	Crew Accommodation	33.	Wheel House and Bridge
25.	Refrigerated Stores	34, 34a.	Derrick Posts, fore and aft

of third time unlucky—when he was in an oil-tanker bound from Sydney for the Persian Gulf, and a Japanese submarine torpedoed her when she was a thousand miles from Colombo. Carpenter was in one of the three lifeboats, which became separated. After sailing for twelve days towards Colombo and covering about five hundred miles the boat he was in was sighted by an American ship, the *Alcoa Pointer*, bound for Fremantle. Later, he heard that the other two boats had taken a month to reach the Maldive Islands. His luck held good for the remainder of the War, and he remained at sea, working for Marconi in various ships until coming to *Northern Star*.

The messages going out from the *Star* started relaying her bad news round the world, and brought representatives of Vickers as well as Parsons and Pametrada to Cape Town. The South Africans gave the new ship a rousing welcome, but there was a taste of ashes in it for MacConochie and Edmeads and Brew and the engineers.

While the passengers went ashore there were post-mortems in the engine-room. During the run to Cape Town the h.p. turbine casings had been lifted, and it was found that damage had been caused to the rotor bladings and stators. They could, however, be repaired. When the ship berthed the two rotors were lifted out of position and crated ready to be flown from Fremantle to Sydney.

What had caused the damage in both turbines? One theory was that the steel lubricating-oil drain-pipes were too rigid.

After the normal stay of one day in Cape Town, *Northern Star* sailed on to Durban, and John and Peggy MacConochie flew back to London. There was no further trouble on the run to Fremantle, where the rotors were flown on to Cockatoo Island. One was waiting when the ship reached Melbourne, and at Sydney the other was ready.

The *Star* stayed for six days at Sydney, instead of the normal two. Both h.p. turbines were reconnected, oil filtered and cleansed, and flexible drain-pipes installed. The thrust collar was machined true. The ship sailed for Wellington with a traditional paper-streamer farewell, and for the first time since that pleasant evening two days out from Las Palmas, Edmeads felt a weight lift from his mind and "Daddy" Brew became more paternal. But the *Star* was late, and in the purser's office and in the offices of the Shaw Savill agents in Sydney, Wellington, and Auckland there had been a vast amount of additional paper-work.

Once past the Sydney Heads, however, life in *Northern Star* settled into routine again. In Wellington and Auckland, New Zealanders gave her a sympathetic welcome, and new passengers settled in for the run to Southampton. They enjoyed Suva and Tahiti and looked forward to Panama. In the engine-room the engineers hovered round the two h.p. turbines. Oil temperatures were taken every fifteen minutes, and logged.

Four days out from Tahiti Brew's telephone rang again.

"Oil temperature on the starboard h.p. thrust up fourteen degrees since the last check, sir."

"Stop the starboard engine," Brew ordered.

Once again the scenes on the Las Palmas–Cape Town run were repeated, for the same damage had recurred. This time the engineers switched to the starboard l.p. turbine in twelve hours. No bolts had to be cut. Their threads had been well lubricated in Sydney.

When the starboard engine was working again Brew

had the port engine stopped and the thrust pads on its h.p. turbine examined. They were wearing, too. Twelve hours later and *Northern Star* was again ploughing on with two half-engines, and the thrust pads were being boxed, ready for flying to England from Panama.

The *Star* had not yet run clear of bad luck for her maiden voyage. Nine days late on the round voyage, she sailed into bad weather on the final lap to Southampton. She was due to berth a 7 A.M., but it was nearer 2 P.M. before she was tied up. Instead of arriving at Waterloo by midday or early afternoon, many passengers did not get to London until nearly 10 P.M.

For Shaw Savill the chief question remained. Could the cause of the wearing of the thrust pads be decided and corrected before the ship was due to sail again?

The pads flown from Panama had been carefully examined, and there were analytical tests. Carbonized iron was found on them. From this discovery positive deductions followed.

One theory was that a chemical action had occurred from the use of excessive pressure oil to lubricate the rotor, made of steel with one-half per cent molybdenum and the white metal lining of the thrust pads. Carbonized iron was formed. Once this hard substance developed it began to cut into the bearing surfaces, causing a rise in temperature which, in turn, increased the formation of the iron.

Whether or not this theory was correct, carbonization was not present when a straight mineral oil was used instead of excessive pressure oil.

Experiments were made during *Northern Star*'s second voyage, but the change of oil seemed to provide answers to the queries that had followed her round the world on her maiden voyage.

There was no further trouble with the h.p. turbines, yet for some time to come the mere mention of e.p. oil and turbines was sufficient to make Brew and his engineers grimace. And for Edmeads to reflect that they had also resulted in another kind of chemical action—the removal of all the gilt from the gingerbread of a maiden voyage, which should have been enjoyable, but was one long toothache.

CHAPTER NINE

Varying Atmospheres

WHEN *Northern Star* began her maiden voyage on July 10th, 1962, almost exactly ten years had passed since the meeting in Leadenhall Street at which it had been agreed that *Southern Cross* should have her engines aft.

The *Star* was now to sail east-about, and the *Cross* to make for Trinidad and Panama, and to circle the globe the other way round. Both were to spend two-thirds of their voyages under the constellation of the Southern Cross and, for a period while they were in the region from the equator to twenty degrees north, to see the Southern Cross and the North Star in the same night sky.

About once a year they were to pass close to each other at sea, travelling in opposite directions.

The first occasion was on March 23rd, 1963, at 7.30 A.M., four days out from Balboa, in the Pacific. Sanderson was aboard the *Star* on a farewell voyage before retiring as chairman, and, when Edmeads and Hopkins brought the ships within two miles of each other, he was on the bridge with his binoculars for a good view of the *Cross* heading for Tahiti. It was a moment to be remembered, this first meeting of the two liners of his own conception. A few days later there was a light-hearted party when the Governor of the Panama Canal Company came aboard and appointed him an honorary pilot, complete with certificate and a token key to the canal locks.

The next meeting of the *Star* and the *Cross* was on February 9th, 1964, at 2.50 P.M., about 430 miles north-east of St Helena, in the Atlantic. Baber was in command of the *Cross*, relieving Hopkins, who was on leave.

Hopkins had been appointed Commodore of the Shaw Savill Line the previous September, succeeding Captain A. C. Jones. He joined the Line thirty-six years before, in November 1927, as fourth officer of the *Tainui*. His training began in 1915, when he went to H.M.S. *Worcester*. Two years later he was a midshipman R.N.R. serving in the cruiser *Shannon*; in 1919 he went to the Orient Line, completed his apprenticeship, and took his master's certificate. He was with Shaw Savill for eleven years before being appointed to his first command, *Waimana*, in February 1948, and he had been master of *Gothic* before following Edmeads in the *Star*.

When the *Cross* and the *Star* met for the second time Edmeads and Baber located each other at 7 A.M. on their direction-finders, 220 miles apart.

The *Cross*, three days out from Cape Town, was one degree to starboard of the *Star*, seven days out from Las Palmas. They kept dead ahead, closing at about forty knots, and picked up each other on their radar screens at a distance of about twenty-eight miles, reporting their respective readings by radio telephone. The ships were visible fifteen miles apart in dull, grey weather, the *Star* forging through thin, rainy mist.

The decks were packed, and cameras and ciné-cameras clicked and whirred as they passed about 500 yards apart, flying the signals "Greetings", followed by "I wish you a pleasant and enjoyable voyage", and "Thank you", the echo of their sirens rolling out over the sea. Their grey hulls and pale-green superstructures, massive above the ocean, were briefly level; then they had passed, and were soon faint grey shapes to each other.

During the morning a leg-puller in the *Cross* posted a notice on the purser's board inviting passengers who wished to be rowed round the *Star* in a lifeboat to put down their names. Several people fell for it, and one inquired at the purser's office about timing and procedure. He received the dead-pan answer that he should apply to the chief steward for a packed lunch. This produced the equally solemn assurance that he should consult the chief officer. The penny dropped, finally.

If it had been possible for anybody to have switched ships in mid-ocean he would have found much the same routine in each, but some difference of atmosphere, for every ship has her own among both passengers and crew. It differs with every voyage, for the passengers are coming and going with each port, and the personnel of the crew is never quite the same.

This atmosphere is known fairly exactly by the captain. Within a short time after a voyage has begun he has an assessment of the types of passengers aboard, the majority of whom fall into well-defined age groups and are content to enjoy the routine of life at sea. A few can be expected to be awkward or complaining over real or imagined grievances, and there are often half a dozen invalids aboard.

The captain has a similar assessment of his officers and crew in the ship's six departments, and of their experience. While the heads of these departments are usually firm fixtures and their number two's have also been several years at sea, there are often frequent changes among the younger officers; and a large number of ratings—particularly stewards and deck hands—are in the ship for one voyage only.

The call of the sea still attracts many men, but there is also a pull from the land in these days of full employment, good pay, and earlier marriages. The wives of young officers don't take kindly to being left four times a year for seventy-six or seven days, and seeing their husbands for a month or two in twelve, and even then in short intervals. The quick turn-round at Southampton, economic though it may be for the Line, also brings human problems. Some of the junior deck officers stay only a short time in one particular vessel, and many engineer officers tend to be at sea for two or three years only, to see the world and to get experience before taking a job ashore.

With a large number of ratings, new to the sea and inexperienced, discipline has necessarily to be strict. The captain has wide powers under the Merchant Shipping Act, and for offences such as drunkenness or absence without leave he is empowered to deduct pay. He deals with offenders at logging sessions, usually held at 10 A.M., and these are sometimes fairly regular after a call at a port. Any serious offences are dealt with ashore by magistrates.

The occasional passenger who steps over the traces is also dealt with, first by the purser, who warns him that another breach will mean being taken before the chief officer, and a third appearing before the captain. The captain may put a passenger ashore at the next port of call and have him brought before a magistrate—in the same way as any member of the crew. The rare passenger who, for instance, may become drunk repeatedly and open the wrong cabin door at night, intentionally or unintentionally, break furniture or cause other damage, could find himself in the ship's 'brig', or lock-up; and if his offence merited being taken before a magistrate he might even remain in the brig until the ship docks.

On some voyages a major concern to the captain and his staff is young women outnumbering the men

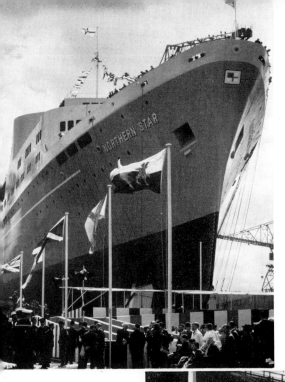

"The great ship . . . resplendent in her fresh grey and light-green paint" (p. 67)

112

By courtesy of Vickers

"The Queen Mother . . . brought fine weather with her" (p. 76)

y courtesy of the Shaw Savill Line

Officer, cadet, and quartermaster in *Northern Star*'s wheelhouse

Northern Star's main boiler

passengers. The ratio has been as high as eight to one on some of the runs, and this can, and occasionally does, lead to differences of opinion among the passengers and crew.

One reason for the atmosphere of every voyage varying is the differing percentages of the age groups. There may be a large number of round-voyage passengers escaping winter months in Britain; there may be a big proportion of the under twenty-fives, particularly going to Britain; there may be a large number of settlers leaving Britain.

The captain knows pretty well all that happens aboard, for, officially and socially, he meets his chief officer, the chief engineer, the purser, catering officer, and the doctor several times a day. They, in turn, are directly in touch with the heads of the branches of their departments as well as with the passengers; and the pattern is repeated all down the ladder. As a system of information of news gathering it is as effective and efficient as any news agency, and as rapid.

The routine of operating the *Cross* and the *Star* is much the same; variations are a matter of personal inclination or habit of the captain. His prime responsibilities are the safety of his passengers and the navigation of his ship. Fire at sea is a lurking hazard, and so is the risk of collision.

The first step to ensure safety before leaving Southampton is crew fire- and boat-drill; every newcomer, especially any at sea for the first time, must know exactly his position and duty when the emergency alarm is sounded.

Many practice drills are held in port, and the day before sailing a surveyor from the Ministry of Transport is invited to attend. All fire and water-tight doors are closed, positions in the ship and at lifeboat muster-stations allotted, all boats on the side opposite to the

s.s.—8

wharf lowered into the water and sailed or rowed, and their provisions and radios checked.

When the passengers come on board the captain has the problem of a large number of people for whose safety he is responsible, and to the majority of whom life at sea is entirely strange. The ship anchors off Cowes Roads for full-scale drills by both passengers and crew lasting about one hour; not until they have been completed does she head for the open sea.

During the voyage crew drills are repeated once a week or as often as the captain and the chief officer think necessary; the drills for passengers are repeated after each batch of new arrivals.

An alarm is sounded, passengers go to their cabins, don their lifebelts, and assemble at their muster-stations opposite a lifeboat. A notice giving the number and position of every passenger's muster-station is posted clearly in every cabin. Members of the crew are encouraged to take a lifeboat drill examination, usually in Wellington, where they must command a lifeboat, operate it away from the ship, and bring it back again under the eye of an examiner. Lifeboats are lowered into the sea at two or three ports during the voyage.

Many passengers tend to regard these drills as a bore, but the order "Abandon ship" has as few attractions now as during the days of the sailing-ships.

At least one elderly lady admitted to Captain Hopkins that she had avoided the drill. When he reproved her for being naughty she was in no way abashed.

"You see, Captain," she said, "if the ship sinks I have no intention of being saved. I shall drown with you."

"Madam," replied Captain Hopkins, "if I have anything to do with it, I have no intention of being drowned."

With an air of shocked surprise she observed, "But surely it is customary."

There was a twinkle in his eye as Captain Hopkins changed the conversation.

He could have told her that navigation is always in the mind of the captain. While the second officer is navigator, the captain must naturally know at all times exactly where his ship is, the state of traffic in the shipping lanes, the distance from the nearest coast, and the time of the next landfall. He is on the bridge while the ship is leaving or arriving in port, on tap to reach it within minutes at any moment of the night or day.

Normally, at sea, the captain's day begins around 7 A.M., when he is called by his "Tiger", or personal steward, responsible for the tidiness of his cabin and sitting-room, dispenser of tea, coffee, and other liquids, according to the hour.

The first report of the day is the ship's "star position", taken each dawn and twilight. Bearings are also checked by the automatic direction-finder, under the control of the chief radio officer, which gives the ship's position from signals sent out continuously by land-based radio stations.

The next report is from the chief officer. He has already been around the ship with the bosun, and talked with the chief steward and the master-at-arms, in charge of the ship's police. Any incidents or complaints are noted and action, if necessary, initiated.

Before going to the second breakfast sitting at 9 A.M. the captain usually walks through the public rooms eyeing their tidiness, and calls on the purser and chief engineer for a run over any events during the night. After breakfast he sees the catering officer for a similar talk, and by the time he returns to his cabin, ready for a logging session, if any, at 10 A.M., he has the feel of the ship. His next call is from the surgeon, who has completed his first surgery and visited any patients who may be in their cabins and not in the hospital.

At eleven o'clock the daily inspection of the ship begins. The officers, in three groups, headed by the captain, chief, and first officers, go round all the passenger accommodation, the public rooms, the cabins, the bathrooms and lavatories, the kitchens, and the storerooms to check that everything is shipshape. Passenger accommodation is inspected four days a week, the crew's on two.

After inspection the heads of all departments assemble to meet the captain, including the refrigeration engineer, who reports on the temperature of the air-conditioning and whether alteration is required. All relevant information about the state of the ship and its atmosphere is pooled, any problems deliberated. Often the purser and catering officer linger on if they have any particular points raised by or about passengers.

At noon the captain receives a check of the ship's position; mileage covered during the past twenty-four hours is recorded and her speed regulated to fit in with her timetable and arrival at the next port.

After lunch the period between two and four o'clock tends to be regarded as siesta time. No public announcements are broadcast. Many of the passengers' deck sports and competitions are held, and officers and crew help with their supervision.

Paper-work keeps the captain occupied between 4 P.M. and 5.30 P.M., and may range from routine reports to the quantity of freshwater being used—it varies according to the latitude and the weather.

Before dinner the captain usually holds a cocktail party, assisted by his senior officers. Guests receive a written invitation. In the *Southern Cross* they are requested to gather on the lounge deck by the large coloured photograph of the Queen, taken when she launched the ship, and in the *Northern Star* by the coloured portrait of the Queen Mother. These are pleasant, informal occasions, part of the process of helping passengers to mix and get to know one another, and, of course, to meet the captain and his officers.

In the same way as the captain, the chief officer has his own routine. He is responsible to the captain for the working of the ship—discipline of the crew, security, repairs, painting, maintenance, the organization for arrival and departures at ports, baggage, the operation of the gangways, the supervision of deck sports of both passengers and crew, and, in the *Star*, the ceremony of crossing the equator. (In the *Southern Cross* the swimming-pool on the deck is not quite large enough for Father Neptune and his cortège.)

The chief officer's heads of branches include the bosun, the carpenter, the plumber, and the master-at-arms, and he sees them regularly. His first round of the ship for the day is at 7 A.M., when he is accompanied by the bosun and runs an eye over the never-ending work of maintenance and repairs. Next he sees the catering officer to note any special programmes for the day, and then the patrol master-at-arms, who reports any incidents during the night. From these conversations he goes on to see the captain.

The purser is next on his list, followed by a meeting with the bosun, the carpenter, and the plumber, when work to be done by the ratings during the day is mapped out and orders given. After this session he gets down to paper-work, which ranges from checking overtime sheets to calculations on the ship's trim and stability. He attends any logging session, takes part in the daily inspections, and goes to the captain's meeting before making his second inspection of the passenger decks at noon. The bosun reports again after lunch, and during the early afternoon there is the supervision of deck sports.

Shortly after four o'clock he discusses with the bosun the routine work for the night watches—the scrubbing of decks between 6 P.M. and 2 A.M. and so on—and then meets the master-at-arms for a quiet contemplation of the ship's atmosphere and, possibly, the behaviour of any of the more extroverted passengers. This is followed by a second set of figures for the day on the soundings of the freshwater tanks and bilges.

The chief officer has regular meetings with the chairman of the crew's social club, of which he is honorary treasurer. The club is formed at the start of each voyage and, normally, is joined by some two-thirds of the ratings. Shaw Savill provides sports equipment. A committee is elected and arranges programmes for the voyage which may range from darts matches and bingo to football matches in ports. The crew's recreation room has its bar—"The Pig and Whistle"—and the evenings are often lively.

The chief engineer's day begins at 7 A.M. with a complete tour of all machinery, starting with the steering gear. He visits the boiler-room, the main engine-room, the generating-room, the air-conditioning room, and the stabilizers. This inspection lasts for at least an hour and a half, and he runs over any problems with the senior second engineer, the chief electrician, the refrigeration engineer, the engine-room storekeeper, and the donkeymen. He relies on the staff chief engineer, his number two, to keep the necessary records and supervise administration.

At noon, after the meeting with the captain and the other heads of departments, the mileage for the past twenty-four hours is worked out, and the number of miles recorded by the engines is compared with the navigator's report. This includes estimating what is known as "the slip". In theory the twin propellers thrust the ship forward nineteen feet with each revolution; but as the months go by after the biennial dry-docking, and the ship's bottom becomes fouled with weeds and barnacles, she does not run so smoothly. As the months proceed the distance the engines are estimated to drive the ship along decreases by a small percentage until, towards the end of the last voyage before dry-docking and scraping, it can tot up to around 8 per cent.

There is a lot of figure-work—checking fuel consumption against horsepower, the daily pumping of fuel-oil from the storing to the settling tanks, filling the storing tanks with distilled water.

Every day, for instance, the *Southern Cross* burns about 100 tons of bunker oil and 10 tons of diesel oil, the latter used by the generators which provide electricity throughout the ship. Bunkering, or re-fuelling, takes place at Las Palmas, Durban, Fremantle, Curaçao, and Trinidad; the price of oil varies.

The *Southern Cross* uses about 180 tons to 220 tons of freshwater each day, the higher figure in the tropics, and the heat in some parts of the engine-room is between 75 and 115 degrees Fahrenheit, also according to latitude. She has about 500 electric motors, each of which has to be checked daily, and control cabins for regulating air-conditioning in the passengers' cabins— a ratio of one for every twelve. Dry heat and humidity are constantly checked with a dry and wet bulb.

The chief electrician, in addition to seeing that the electrical system never fails, has to ensure that all the telephones are working—there are over forty in key positions—and the lifts. Attendants had to be put on in the *Northern Star* when children discovered an additional game—one team in the lifts racing another running up the stairs.

The chief radio officer and his four officers, all employed and seconded by Marconi, whose equipment they operate, have a similar variety of responsibilities. There is the running of the navigational instruments —the automatic direction-finder, the radar screen, and the echo-sounder, or seagraph, which measures the depth of water under the keel to 630 fathoms.

There is the sound recording equipment, which relays announcements to all parts of the ship. No fewer than six different programmes can be distributed simultaneously—a music recital to the forward lounge, dance music to the cinema-ballroom, and dance music to the Tavern. Any or all of these programmes can be 'over-ridden' at any time if announcements should be necessary from the bridge, the deck, or the purser's office.

There is also the receiving and sending of radio messages for the ship's and passengers' official and personal business. Daily contact is kept with Portishead, the United Kingdom station sending messages to long-distance ships, and also with ports all along the route. They may range from requests by the purser for aircraft or railway bookings to birthday greetings and presents to relatives and friends ashore—and the presents ordered may be anything from flowers and nylon stockings to book and gramophone-record tokens. A ship's letter-telegram costs ten shillings for twenty words and is usually delivered within two days; the rate for immediate delivery is one shilling and eight-pence a word.

News is also picked up by the radio-room every day. The BBC is tape-recorded and relayed in the cinema lounge at 5.30 P.M. News-agency reports are recorded—Reuters from Rugby, the Australian Associated Press from Sydney, and the New Zealand Press Association from Wellington. A news sheet is edited and stencilled and run off by the printer every morning; it contains between three and five thousand words, and covers international news, sport, and Stock Exchange prices.

A continuous watch is kept for distress signals on the distress-call frequency—five hundred kilocycles. For three minutes on the half-hour every ship observes a radio silence. Several frequencies are used for messages—medium for distances up to four to five hundred miles, and high frequencies for long distances. Different megacycle bands are used according to the time of day.

The chief radio officer is also responsible for seeing that the transmitting and receiving radio-sets in two lifeboats are always in working order, as well as a portable transmitter-receiver. On high frequency these sets can send and receive over distances of a thousand miles.

In *Northern Star* the radio officers also supervise two daily television programmes, relayed over closed circuits to a dozen sets—for children in the afternoon and adults in the evening. A library of films is kept, sufficient for the run from Southampton to Sydney; on the homeward run the programmes are repeated. 'Telly' is just as popular afloat as ashore; it is picked up live in port.

Incidents, and methods of dealing with them, become part of the routine for the captain and his officers.

They include the handling of the occasional stowaway who may imagine that when he is discovered he will be landed at the port he has in mind. If he does believe this he is in for a shock, for a stowaway is usually brought back to the port where he came aboard and can be taken before a magistrate.

Every stowaway has to be questioned about his

birthplace, his next-of-kin, his last job, and so on, because normally he will have no papers on him, and probably no money either. Immigration officials in ports throughout the world are wary of permitting a stowaway to land unless it can be firmly established that he has a right to do so by reason of nationality. Shipping lines can be put to considerable expense, because a stowaway has to be accommodated and fed on board until he is allowed ashore.

The average stowaway is tractable, and accepts the consequences of his position. One or two are awkward.

A tall, truculent Australian was found wandering round the *Southern Cross* by the master-at-arms late at night after sailing. He refused to answer questions and to give any information about himself. He was taken before Baber, and he continued to be truculent and uninformative.

"Master-at-arms," Baber said curtly, "are you and I the only two people on board who know this man is in the ship?"

"Yes, sir."

"Then throw him overboard," said Baber.

The Australian took a quick glance at the two impassive faces—and wilted. There was no further trouble with him after this successful bluff, and he did not leave Australia.

Not all stowaways are men. At Las Palmas a woman blithely gave a name and a cabin number to the duty officer and the master-at-arms at the gangway when she came aboard the *Southern Cross* just before sailing-time; although they were doubtful of her, one of the officers was certain he had danced with her during the run from Southampton. After the ship sailed, however, the purser's office reported that no passenger of the name she had given was in the cabin she had selected.

This was not the extent of her inaccurate information; she believed the *Southern Cross* was sailing for Southampton. In fact, the next port was Cape Town, where she was landed and sent back to Las Palmas.

Another additional passenger not on the purser's list was once discovered in the ladies' cloakroom— a new-born baby. The problem was to find the mother. Inquiries were discreet; nobody was anxious to ask any woman aboard whether she had had a baby lately. But there were suspicions about an Australian girl. When the ship arrived at Sydney she was confronted by women police. She admitted that she was the mother and had delivered the child herself.

Occasionally somebody jumps overboard. Suicidal tendencies are not uncommon, and there have been cases—not restricted to Shaw Savill ships—of passengers disappearing in the night. On one occasion a steward went round the public rooms declaring that he was going to jump and inviting company for immersion. He was not taken seriously—until he did throw himself over, and quickly shouted and waved for help.

On the bridge the officer in charge ordered the helmsman to turn hard a-port. When a half-circle was completed he gave the order "Hard a-starboard." The helmsman misunderstood, thinking the turn to port should be continued. This delayed the rescue by four minutes. Even so, the steward was out of the water thirty-five minutes after he had jumped.

Sometimes there are tragedies. At Trinidad an assistant bosun helping to lower a gangway was caught up in the ropes, which circled his neck. He was hanged before he could be cut free. When the passengers learned that he had left a widow and children, including a spastic, they collected £1000 to be added to the Line's compensation.

An understanding of human nature and its vagaries is common to most of the senior staff and is soon developed by the younger members. Many of the older officers have been through the mill themselves and have vivid memories, particularly those at sea during the War.

The chief radio officer in the *Southern Cross*, for instance, Donald MacRae, another Scot, the son of a stationmaster on the old Highland railway at Conan Bridge, Ross-shire, went to sea during the First World War after he had failed to bluff his way into the Army at the age of fifteen and a half.

He has been in three torpedoed ships. One was *Athenia*, hit six hours after the Second World War was declared, off the north-west coast of Ireland. She was filled with passengers, and MacRae, as second radio officer, was ordered into a lifeboat fitted with a radio transmitter. He had no opportunity to use it, for he was obliged to take command of the boat and keep the survivors as cheerful as possible until they, with some four hundred other passengers were picked up by a Norwegian cargo-ship.

Among the officers nearly a generation younger than MacRae is the staff chief engineer in the *Northern Star*, W. Woods, whose father was a fitter and moved from Manchester to Woolwich, in London. Woods won a scholarship to Woolwich Technical College, spent his five years in an engineering apprenticeship at the Royal Ordance factory, and became a fitter and then a tool-maker until he joined the Union Castle Line.

He was in *Landaff Castle* when she was torpedoed in the Indian Ocean about ninety miles from the South African coast, and came up from the boiler-room after it had been hit on the starboard side and the main engine stopped through lack of steam. All the launchable lifeboats were away, and, with other engineers, he went round throwing rafts overboard. He was flattened by a column of water spouting when a second torpedo arrived, and decided that it was time to jump and make for a raft. From one of these he clambered into a boat in time to see a third torpedo break the ship in two. Only one man went down in her—the barman, who had returned for his takings.

It was dusk when the German submarine surfaced, the conning-tower opened, and an officer appeared and stood under a spotlight, hands behind his back.

"What is the name of this ship?" he shouted to the lifeboats.

"*The Lagoona Belle*," yelled a derisive Cockney, with memories of the run down the Thames to Southend.

The German moved his hands from behind his back, and pointed a tommy-gun in the direction of the Cockney.

"What ship?" he asked, ominously.

"*Landaff Castle*," yelled a number of voices.

"You have food and water?"

"Yes."

"Well, this is your position. . . ."

Two days later Woods and the other survivors were picked up by the destroyer *Inconstant* and taken to Durban.

The generation which has gone to sea since the War has found employment easier and less eventful. Typical of those now emerging as potential captains, younger than Baber by ten years, are Reid and also Ian Cameron, chief officer in the *Southern Cross*.

Cameron's family has a Merchant Navy background. His father, J. M. Cameron, was master of *Mahana* for seventeen years, and his maternal grandfather, a Norwegian, was an owner and shipmaster. Ian Cameron was educated at Eastbourne College and the Southampton School of Navigation, and joined Shaw Savill in 1949 at the age of eighteen. His promotion has been regular.

There has been a steady improvement in the conditions of life at sea. There is more comfort, more space, the food is better, air-conditioning sucks out ship smells and aids a good night's sleep in the tropics.

There is, naturally, a turning of thoughts to land and to home, and among the crew of *Southern Cross* this has taken a positive form—the 'adoption' of Vale Road School for physically handicapped children at Tottenham, London.

Some of the crew write regularly to the children, some crippled, others paralysed, telling them of the world outside Vale Road, of the ports at which *Southern Cross* calls. And every December, when the ship is in Southampton just before Christmas, a party is held aboard for the children by the crew, who give up a day or two of their limited time in England to entertain them.

A special box is kept in *Southern Cross* in which the crew drop loose coins from their pay to build up a fund to buy gifts. When the ship was at home in August 1964 there was sufficient saved to provide the school with a minibus. The presentation was made on behalf of the crew by Cameron, the chief officer, and to the delight of the children the Mayoress of Tottenham, Mrs A. J. Protheroe, christened the bus *Southern Cross* with champagne which bubbled and then trickled over a coloured plaque showing the constellation on the side of the bus. The Middlesex County Council indicated its appreciation by agreeing to contribute £150 a year towards running costs.

The school now has a daily reminder of *Southern Cross*, whose progress round the world is charted as thoroughly at Vale Road as it is in Leadenhall Street.

CHAPTER TEN

"So the Days drift by . . ."

THE ship nods gently towards the horizon
rather like an old man following a long conversation very slowly. The sun blazes from the
blue bowl of the sky, and the restless sea glitters and
winks, a wilderness of lively water. A continuous soft
splash of waves, as they leap and surge away from the
hull, mingles drowsily with the steady hum of
machinery. A caressing breeze flirts over the decks,
and fans away the bite of the sun from the brown
flesh of passengers as they lie and loll and bask and
read or chat, or are busy about their deck sports.

This is life at its most pleasant during the longer
runs between ports, when the days pass in a set
pattern and time slips by as easily as the ocean. These
are the best-remembered days of a voyage and, in
memory, efface phases when grey or black clouds
blot out the sun, the sea is dark, forbidding, and
threatening, and wind slashes like an icy whip or
drives a stinging, cold rain; or when the air is as heavy
and humid as a soft, damp, oppressive sheet, clinging
and sweaty.

The scene varies from day to day, sometimes from
hour to hour; but the setting remains constant.

Passengers soon settle into a routine punctuated by
meal-times.

Their day begins when their steward brings tea and
biscuits shortly before seven o'clock and, in the

centre-line cabins with no portholes, the circular yellow globe of the artificial sun begins to glow for an hour.

The cabin steward is one of the two men on the staff whom they see most regularly—the other is their restaurant steward—whose personalities and efficiency influence the enjoyment of a voyage.

The cabin steward can be a mine of useful information —about the ship and its life, about ports and places to visit. The saloon steward, if he is quick and intelligent, makes the difference between an enjoyable meal or one which is a series of long pauses with food arriving half cold and indifferently served. As human nature varies, so do stewards and their attitude to their jobs; invariably the older and more mature, who are accustomed to life at sea, are those most appreciated.

Other stewards whom passengers get to know are in the lounges, the Tavern, and the bars. Normally, like the cabin stewards on the upper decks, they are mature, patient, understanding. In the Tavern their work is often concentrated.

The first meal of the day is for the children up to the age of twelve. Their breakfast and lunch is three-quarters of an hour before the first sittings, dinner an hour before. The service for children is a feature of both ships. They have their own special deck areas and rooms and swimming-pools, and are not allowed in the lounges, the Tavern, or on the sports deck (unless they have their own competitions).

"We need never see them," say some parents, particularly those of older children.

Naturally the number is never the same, and the children's hostesses have their hands rather more than full on some voyages.

During the hour or so between the stewards arriving with tea and biscuits and the gong for the first breakfast

By courtesy of the Shaw Savill Line

"The receiving and sending of radio messages" (p. 120)

"The captain must know at all times exactly where his ship is" (p. 115)

By courtesy of the Shaw Savill Line

Northern Star's swimming
pool . . . is popular wher
ever the sun is burnin
down (p. 131)

Southern Cross — "quoi
are sliding along the pitch
rubber rings flipping o
deck-tennis nets" (p. 130

By courtesy of the Shaw Savill I

129

By courtesy of K. E. Niven, I

sitting the swimming-pools attract the energetic; morning constitutionals are more popular.

Sittings and table seatings are allotted by the purser's staff and the second stewards in charge of the restaurants, with whom changes may be arranged. Officers have their own tables, usually at the second sittings. The seating, including that at the captain's table, is influenced by a list of what are known as 'commended' people who may be prominent in public or business life; but there is nothing arbitrary about it, and the second stewards see that there is a leavening of age groups.

Round about the time the first breakfast gong beats out its notes a public announcement from the purser's office gives the day, the date, the weather forecast, the position of the ship, any main items of world news, and the programme for sports and entertainments for the day.

Some passengers pay more attention to it than others. When one of the younger pursers announced in the *Southern Cross* that she was sailing through a sea 6000 fathoms deep he added, "If you put Everest, Snowdon, and Ben Nevis on top of one another, that will give you some idea of our height above the ocean floor." Later that morning when the library opened an enthusiastic statistician was waiting; within a short time he was on his way to the purser's office with a correction. The morning's announcement, he said, included an error of a thousand feet.

At nine o'clock the gong sounds for the second breakfast sitting, and the ship is now fully awake. In the *Northern Star* the launderette, with its twelve washing-machines and six tumbler dryers, becomes busy, and there is a ripple of ship's gossip—a theory is that a concealed microphone would convey an interesting and accurate assessment of the atmosphere aboard.

9

The purser's office, the mail office, the shop, and the hairdressing saloons are open. There is a browsing round to read notices, to order photographs taken by the ship's photographer. On the decks favourite niches are being sought and deck-chairs—provided free—appropriated. Quoits are sliding along the pitches, rubber rings flipping over deck-tennis nets, and there is a constant clicking from the table-tennis area by the Tavern.

Sports competitions are arranged for each long run, and there are men's, women's, and mixed doubles competitions for deck quoits and tennis. Netball is popular, and there is a national note about the tug-o'-war and deck cricket, the women of "England" pulling against the women of "South Africa", and "M.C.C." batting against "Australia", "New Zealand", or "Rhodesia". All are keenly contested, and the finals watched by quite big gatherings.

Deck cricket is popular with both men and women, and in the *Southern Cross* the winners of the men's knock-out are challenged by the officers, a match started somewhat tentatively by Baber and Cameron. (The officers have their own sports, notably deck-tennis singles, which can be as strenuous as squash or badminton.)

The cricket "finals" are given a light-hearted touch by both teams appearing in fancy dress—the officers as "Old Hambledonians", complete with black paper top-hats, flowing beards and whiskers, and coloured waistcoats; the Australians as bushrangers, and the New Zealanders as Maoris.

The cricket is not quite as it is known at Lord's or Headingley, or even the village green for that matter. The ball is cork or wood and not always round, the stumps are on springs, the bat half-size. Chalk-lines are drawn on the deck and numbered "one", "two", and "four" for the scoring, and every man in the team bowls. The bounce of the ball is awkward to gauge, wides are frequent, and often an innings does not rise much above fifty or sixty. Any carefree batsman hitting the ball into the sea loses his team twenty runs. The bosun takes a hand, slipping the bowler the occasional bread-roll, orange, potato, boiled egg, and perhaps a balloon filled with water. It is all fun and does nothing to reduce the zest to win.

In the *Northern Star* the lido with its large swimming-pool—thirty feet by twenty-two feet—and mosaic tiling on the walks is popular whenever the sun is burning down, and is usually packed by so many sunbathers that it looks like the famous Bondi beach, and some of the figures on display are attractive and shapely. The main pool is flanked on either side by a non-swimmers' pool and a paddling-pool; and a soda fountain is rarely without customers.

"Crossing the Line" ceremonies take place at the main pool, the passengers volunteering for the roles of Neptune and his minions, aided by a loudspeaker and the ship's band. All the traditions are observed, the shavings are energetic, the duckings thorough, and there are usually one or two gratuitous immersions, with the hostess being flung in as a matter of form. Normally this ceremony and the final of the cricket competition are during the afternoon.

The bars open in the morning at eleven o'clock in the Tavern and lounges and add a pleasant atmosphere of relaxation after any rigours of the deck; the band alternates on different days in the lounges. The bars close at 2 P.M. until 5 P.M., when they remain open until 10.30 or 11 P.M.

During the morning tickets for the tote on the ship's daily run are sold by volunteers for sixpence each; the figure is announced shortly after noon, and the winning tickets are usually worth a few pounds. The odds have been worked out by the purser's office.

After the luncheon sittings siestas may be interrupted for a variety of entertainment in addition to deck sports. The contract-bridge players, for instance, soon collect after leaving port for a progressive competition organized by the hostess and to form partnerships for the main knock-out competition; the tables seem to be in use throughout the day and the evenings. The chess players also have a knock-out competition, and settle to their brow-furrowed concentration in the lounges, the library, or perhaps in the sun on the decks.

The children's sports have the usual complications of rope obstacles, buns on strings, apples in water-buckets, and their fancy-dress parade in the cinema is colourful and the result of much parental thought and work.

For those who like to relax to classical music special concerts are arranged, when music is relayed either from a record-player or from a tape-recorder and played back to the passengers over high-fidelity loudspeakers.

Those who enjoy their tea in the mornings and evenings pay a small amount. Charges are made only for tea, coffee, ice-cream, and—at night—for hot dogs in the Tavern.

As the time for the final meal 'punctuation' of the day approaches—the two dinner sessions—there is a drift to change from shorts and sports wear. The majority of men don lounge suits, and some who are going to the captain's party may match the officers' evening dress with dinner suits—if they have re-membered to bring them.

There is a different programme each night—a film show, bingo, a quiz, a dance, or a race meeting on deck, after which fish and chips are served, wrapped in traditional newspapers. A fancy-dress dance sees about one-third of the passengers competing, and about the same percentage for a mad hatters' ball. The standard is invariably high, the product of imagination and hard work. One winning fancy dress in the *Southern Cross* was "Passing Waves"—cardboard models of the *Southern Cross* and the *Northern Star*; the second prize went to "Lofty", a man wearing a large paper top-hat which covered his chest.

Landfall dinners are held two nights before reaching port after the longer runs, when the restaurants are decorated and paper hats are the rig of the night; they are followed by a dance in the cinema lounge which may be, and sometimes is, continued until the wee sma' 'oors in the Tavern, where there is dancing every night, anyway.

So the days drift by, spent lazily or energetically, influenced like all holidays by the weather, when time is unimportant, there are no telephones—the martinets of modern life—and the worries of life in cities and towns and villages are dim and distant memories . . . there is little or nothing that can be done about them. International crises seem academic.

It has been said that what is real at sea is unreal on land, and what is real on land is unreal at sea. Whether or not this is true, personal likes and dislikes can become intensified, friendships develop quickly, and after a few days seem to have lasted for years; personal dislikes may become sharp and sudden, and minor irritations a cause for major annoyance.

There is a mixed diet of people and personalities in a one-class tourist ship, with a wide range of professions and backgrounds and incomes. In the main the tendency—in addition to a rough self-sorting out of age groups to the different lounges and the Tavern—

is for the individual to gravitate to a small group and
to have a number of nodding acquaintances outside it.
People are still making new acquaintances a fortnight
after embarking. Some are quiet and keep to themselves, others are gregarious, some are extroverts.
Inevitably each voyage seems to produce a ship's bore,
a crack-hearty humorist, and a 'bar-propper'.

There is also the occasional 'character'. An Australian swaggie, or tramp, boarded the *Northern Star*
in Sydney and was suspected of being a stowaway
until he produced a ticket for a three-berth cabin. His
companions were somewhat put out when he refused
to undress when going to bed and clambered between
the sheets with his boots on. They mentioned his habits
to the catering officer; the swaggie still refused to remove his boots, and was shepherded to a single cabin.

The following morning an alarmed lounge steward
reported that the Australian was boiling his billy over
a fire made from newspapers. Flames were leaping a
foot high. When the catering officer had the fire doused
promptly, the swaggie was pained. It was the only
way to make a good cup of tea, he declared.

There were other incidents on the way to Southampton, where the Australian landed as unkempt and
untidy as he had boarded in Sydney. He would not
have won a prize for the most popular person aboard,
and the passenger department in Leadenhall Street
was told that the *Northern Star* did not want to take
him back to Sydney.

The ship completed another round voyage, and when
it next sailed from Southampton one of the first
passengers up the gangway was the Australian, un-
recognized after his stay of nearly three months in
England. Now he was wearing a smart new suit and
polished shoes, and there were pyjamas in his suitcase.
By the time he reached Sydney he was one of the most

popular passengers, and took first prize as Burlington
Bertie at the fancy-dress dance. He admitted that his
conversion was the result of his reception in London.
No hotel would accept him at first, and he had slept
in Hyde Park and had not appreciated snow and bitter
weather.

Some elderly people travel regularly. One woman
explained her reasons this way: "My husband is dead,
my family grown-up, and I don't care to live alone.
I don't like living in a hotel, where I'm just another
old woman and nobody takes any particular interest
in me. But in a ship I always find somebody to talk
with and be friends. I always have company, and if
I'm not well I know I can get medical attention
quickly. There is something to do each day and in the
evenings. There is always the next port to look forward
to. I don't have to be worried about anything. It is
much better for me than being in a hotel."

Passengers' queries and complaints are infinite in
their variety.

"Why is it that I never hear a bird singing at sea?"
one woman inquired in the *Northern Star.*

Another wanted to know what kind of machinery in
the swimming-pool made the water move from side
to side.

One bearded Sanderson during his farewell voyage.

"Why can't you do something about these long
stretches of ten days at sea?" he demanded. "Why
can't we visit ports more often. Look at the run from
Durban to Fremantle—nine solid days with absolutely
nothing to do. It's not good enough."

Sanderson regarded him gravely.

"The trouble is," he said, "that when the good Lord
made the Indian Ocean He didn't consult us."

As for complaints about the food, there may be one
or two at the start of a voyage before the routine in the

kitchens has settled down and the new stewards have learned their jobs. The main problem of the chef is to make mass-prepared food taste like home meals. On an average round voyage the *Northern Star* serves something like 136,000 meals, and a small percentage of these may be criticized. But after every voyage the company receives many complimentary letters from passengers about the food.

Every year girls from South Africa, Australia, and New Zealand go to England in droves to take jobs and travel round Britain and on the Continent. They remain for quite long periods, often up to two years, and some—like the younger men aboard—have little money and only a vague idea of the jobs they will find when they land. Some do secretarial work, others work in shops and stores, or in restaurants and bars. Some are nurses, others are going to study. Most are just wanting to see something of the world before settling down. "What girl doesn't hope for romance at sea?" said one girl.

Most of the single men seem to have more of a set purpose—to study, to seek further experience in their jobs, or believe that they may find more scope in Britain than in their home countries. Whatever the purpose of travelling, there is a constant mingling of Commonwealth peoples, which results in varying degrees of "Commonwealth understanding". Sometimes it leaves them unsettled. Some people, after returning home, want to be back in Britain; others after coming to Britain would prefer to be back in the lands where there is more sunshine and a greater sense of personal freedom.

Passengers soon become immersed in their own affairs, with deck games, with bridge, or reading, or seeing over the bridge or the engine-room, and looking forward to the next port.

They may attend the official half-hour Sunday-morning church service in the central lounge, taken by the captain and the purser. Hymns are sung with tremendous cheerfulness; the service, indeed, is one of the most popular of the ship's events.

Most enjoy a "long sea voyage", the routine, the relaxation, the new friendships, the rambling conversations, the changing scene, the restlessness of the sea, the sun and fresh air, and the anticipation of eventual arrival. Even though many may not be sorry when the time comes to leave the ship, they will have a sense of nostalgia, and welcome the sight of the ship again, or read about her with something of a possessive interest. They will forget any irritations, minor or major, remember the people they liked, the laughter and the humorous incidents, and the places they have seen. Most of them—if they had the money and the time and perhaps the purpose—would welcome another voyage; and make all the same complaints and afterwards retain the same pleasant memories.

"I can take any amount of the life at sea," said a New Zealander, musing over a voyage in the *Northern Star*. "Just lead me to it."

CHAPTER ELEVEN

"See the Purser"

SEE the purser" is the advice given passengers wanting information. Translated this means "Ask at the purser's office", where his staff has a list of duties ranging from checking passports and tickets, cashing cheques and receiving messages to be cabled, to wrapping prizes for presentation by the captain in the forward lounge after the landfall dinners.

In *Northern Star*, Oliver, the Line's senior purser, who has been at sea for thirty-six years and in both *Southern Cross* and *Northern Star* for their maiden voyages, has a deputy, a second purser, three third pursers, a purserette, and two writers. In *Southern Cross*, Bickell, also in both ships for their maiden voyages and promoted from deputy at the beginning of 1964, has a similar staff, but two purserettes instead of one.

The responsibilites are many, and not the least is handling around £200,000 in cash every voyage, including some £50,000 in travellers' cheques. Mail also comes under the department and keeps one of the writers busy full-time; he will sell about £700 worth of sixpenny British air letters each voyage in *Northern Star*, and in *Southern Cross* the sales will tot up to some £500. There is also a vast amount of documentation.

All this is very different from the days when Oliver became an assistant purser in *Hobson's Bay* in 1931 and was half the staff. While the purser had his own duties, Oliver would work all day in the office either at the counter with passengers, looking after the cash, or manifesting cargo, and typing away at passenger lists for two or three hours every evening.

It was not his first job. A Londoner, he was educated at Ealing, and when work was scarce in 1925 he ran messages for a lawyer and polished the brass plate while waiting for an opening as office-boy in the Commonwealth Line in Australia House. There he worked in a basement under the Strand in a former coal-cellar, which still had a circular pavement grating, and sent off tickets and labels and looked after the filing. He drew 15s. a week until his promotion to the traffic department after eighteen months. A year or so later he moved again when the Commonwealth Line was bought by Shaw Savill; he was transferred to Leadenhall Street and the Australian outward freight department, and there he decided that he would like to try life at sea instead of in the City of London. His chance came when an assistant purser resigned, and he joined *Hobson's Bay.*

Bickell, born and educated in Bristol, went to sea when he came of age just before the War began, and was in *Monarch of Bermuda*, used as a troop carrier, throughout hostilities. He joined Shaw Savill in 1949 after a period with Furness Withy. He was in *Southern Cross* until 1960, when he moved to *Dominion Monarch* for her final voyages, and then rejoined Oliver in *Northern Star.*

Just as Brew and Jones and Worden and their engineers sometimes have 'troubles' in the engine-room, so Oliver and Bickell and their staffs have problems among the passengers.

"Many people are travelling to or away from a problem," says Oliver, who is stocky and greying, and who draws away at a cigarette-holder as thoughtfully as Edmeads. "People always travel for a purpose, even round-voyagers. The reasons why they travel are infinite."

As seen from the purser's office, not everybody goes aboard cheerful and relaxed and looking forward to the voyage. Many brood over whether they have made the right decision, perhaps to uproot themselves and settle in another country; others may be returning home and are wondering whether in fact they want to go home. They may be homesick already, as well as sad at leaving friends and relatives, not knowing when they will see them again. There is usually an atmosphere of uncertainty during the first three or four days, particularly after sailing from Southampton, when it is easy to discover that some of the passengers are ready to say they dislike everything about the ship—the cabins, the food, the public rooms—and grumble about the staff. Some become seasick and are miserable, and there are a few who say they are going to leave the ship at Las Palmas and return to England.

Las Palmas seems to settle them down. They go ashore, shop, and see a foreign land—many for the first time—and when they get back to the ship it is with something of a sense of returning home, of finding that what was strange and new only a day or so ago is now a place filled with faces they know and with people to look after them. When the ship sails for Cape Town they seek out the niches they had already tentatively earmarked for themselves, and begin to relax and to realize that, whether they have been right or wrong about travelling, there is nothing they can do about it now, and that they may just as well enjoy themselves, before again facing up to their problems ten days, three weeks, or a month ahead.

"By the time they leave the ship for the last time you probably find that about 70 per cent have a feeling of

sadness," says Oliver. "Even though they may criticize
her, she has been a home, and they're bound to have
made friends whom they will probably never see
again. They're most likely to be fitter after their
holiday and feel more able to cope with their worries."

From the purser's point of view there is no set
pattern about dealing with passengers' complaints,
which differ with every individual—except that understanding, tact, and patience are needed. Some people
burst in on the purser in his private office, bang the
table, and threaten. Some are polite, others shy, others
again timid but firm. Often the noisiest are the easiest
to deal with; they may have wanted to complain almost
for the sake of complaining, and having done so and
got it off their chests they feel better about it. Dealing
with them is just one part of the day's work for the
purser and his staff.

There is a vast amount of paper-work. Some of the
staff are engaged on work for the Governments of the
countries lying ahead rather than for Shaw Savill. On
the run to Cape Town information required by the
South African Government has to be prepared—
customs papers, passenger lists, and so on. Similar
work for the Australian Government continues between
Durban and Fremantle, and across the Tasman to
Wellington for the New Zealand Government. The
United Kingdom requires the least 'paper' of any
Government.

Every port means work. Passengers will be disembarking—as many as five hundred at Durban, and
seven hundred in Wellington—and others will be
going on tours. Many inquire about rail and air
services and require bookings. The crew will want
advances on their pay. The mail has to be sorted and
placed on tables in the forward lounge alphabetically.
If everything goes well and the ship, the pilot, and the

customs and migration officers are all on time, then it is a matter more or less of routine. But if timings are awry frustrations can mount.

Dealing with cash requirements of both passengers and crew keeps the office busy. At sea there is a steady cashing of travellers' cheques for spending in the bars and the shop; on a round voyage the bars will take about £22,000 and the shop slightly more, perhaps £24,000 or so. For some reason the takings at both are roughly equal, the amount spent on cameras, films, pens, and a wide range of presents and souvenirs matching the sum handed over for spirits, beer, and cigarettes.

Before arrival at a port the purser's office may have to pay out anything up to £10,000 and more if, for instance, a thousand or so of the passengers decide to spend £10 ashore. If spending is heavy it may be necessary for the purser to cash ashore a proportion of travellers' cheques which have been accepted; if spending is light and his bank is getting rather full he may deposit a sum for the sister ship to collect when she arrives a few days or weeks later. If he is running short he cables ahead to the Line's agents to bring cash aboard.

There are special arrangements for the crew. In *Northern Star* their wages amount to about £1500 a day or £115,000 a voyage, or nearly 38 per cent of total running costs. Every member may have allotments deducted at fortnightly or monthly intervals and paid either to relatives or into a banking account. Their expenses during the voyage, such as for insurance, taxation, or tobacco and spirits, are deducted, as well as any advances at ports. This work is calculated mechanically. On returning to Southampton after a voyage everyone is paid in cash up to midnight on the day of arrival. If the ship is late another day's pay has to be divided up and added to each packet. Whatever the amount of cash in the purser's office a sum sufficient to pay the crew is always taken aboard the ship in port.

The purser's office opens at 9 A.M., closes during the luncheon sittings, and its afternoon session ends at 5 or 5.30 P.M. Any passengers wanting to see the purser personally are received in his private office between 10 and 11 A.M. This is followed by the morning inspection and the heads-of-staff meeting with the captain. All deck sports and evening entertainments are supervised from his main office, and his staff will run the bingo sessions and compère the dances.

Every passenger probably calls at the office several times during a voyage, and since on a round voyage, with passengers disembarking and embarking at the various ports, there may be a 'turnover' of around three thousand people, the staff has a good insight into human nature and its infinite permutations. Requests vary from the changing of a cabin or the stapling of a broken strap of a camera to the seeking of a lost cardigan. People often become careless with their possessions at sea, and although notices are posted when clothing is found, it is not unusual for a few sackloads of lost property to be sent from Southampton to London at the end of a voyage. On the other hand, stealing is rare.

One of the purser's problems is providing entertainment to appeal to people of all ages, from the old to the very young. There can be complaints from the various age groups if an appropriate balance is not kept. Here he is assisted by the hostess, who arranges a "Woman's Hour" and talks or lectures, and who encourages the shy and the retiring to make friends and take part in the sports and entertainments.

"There are all sorts of problems," says Oliver, as he puffs away at his cigarette. "But I suppose the main headache is keeping to schedule. You realize, when you are in *Southern Cross* and *Northern Star*, how the world has changed from the old days. The speed of living is faster.

"At one time passenger-ships did not necessarily keep to schedule, because they hadn't the reserve of speed to pick up time. Nobody was particularly worried. But now it is important that we should try to arrive on the dot. Passengers know they will land at a certain time on a certain day, and they make all their arrangements ahead. If we are late, then the whole world falls round our ears.

"This happens very rarely. I think the only time we were late in *Southern Cross* was on her fourth voyage. We ran into a northerly gale on leaving Las Palmas, and Sir David Aitchison kept going at a maximum practical speed. But after twenty-four hours it was plain that we should be late at Southampton if the gale kept up. Sir David radioed London so that the pilot and the customs people could be told, and the train times altered. A few hours after the message had gone the *Cross* ran into blue skies and calm sea. We could have been on time after all, but it was too late then to make another change."

Oliver does not subscribe to the comment of some pursers: "People are divided into three categories— men, women, and passengers."

"I like dealing with people," he says. "I think it's a challenge when you are sent away with 1400 people and told to land them in good shape and saying they have enjoyed the voyage."

CHAPTER TWELVE

A Double Set of Problems

TWO men for whom life is real, earnest, and seldom a laughing matter in either the *Star* or the *Cross* are the catering officers. It is their responsibility to see that the passengers are well fed and the cabins and public rooms are kept tidy. Their departments have the biggest number of ratings in the ships, and their duties range from working out menus a week in advance of every meal to buying potatoes in the cheapest markets along the route.

In *Northern Star* Browne, short, rotund, is rather like a grave Mr Pickwick. He began his career in catering when he was sixteen, and left Southampton, where he was born and educated, the son of a master-builder, for the only catering school he had heard of in 1927, a French establishment in Lausanne. He borrowed the fare from his father, and was set to work scrubbing kitchen floors and helping the cooks. Three years later, fluent in French, he signed on as an assistant steward in the Canadian Pacific's *Empress of Australia,* and remained with the company until 1946. He was in several of its ships, including the *Duchess of Atholl* when she was torpedoed three days out from Cape Town, and the *Duchess of Richmond* when she was bombed near Gibraltar. The bomb had a time fuse, which was fortunate since it ended up in his cabin—while he was in it.

"I had a job to get out; it was blocking the door,"

he complains. "But it was just as well it stuck there—another five inches or so and it would have gone straight down to the engine-room."

For three years after leaving Canadian Pacific Browne was a relieving manager in Southampton and Portsmouth hotels—until he became bored. "There was not enough to do," he says.

He joined Shaw Savill in 1949 as staff chief steward in *Dominion Monarch* until he moved on to *Southern Cross* for her maiden voyage; he was nearly two years at Walker-on-Tyne watching over the planning and equipping of the kitchens in *Northern Star*.

Catering for both ships is a major operation. Orders for food for the following voyage are sent to Leadenhall Street by *Northern Star* from Panama and *Southern Cross* from Cape Town before they begin the final run to Southampton, where supplies are delivered by the shore staff superintendents. There is a storing programme for each day of the turn-round; and when the ships are in port for only a week work goes on twenty-four hours a day. The bulk of the buying is in England, and additional supplies are bought along the route—tomatoes in Las Palmas, fruit in Cape Town, butter and meat in Australia and New Zealand.

"We buy the best quality and watch the markets," says Browne. "For instance, in some ports potatoes have on occasions been £100 a ton. But if we can get them for £30 a ton in South Africa and £20 a ton in Australia, naturally we cable ahead and buy as we go along."

Three of the catering officer's six departments—the chefs, the store-keepers, and the butchers and bakers—are highly specialized. Menus are worked out with the head chef so that food is taken out of the freezers and thawed slowly—meat, for example, which is prepared by the butcher and his staff for the kitchen.

"The kitchens in both ships are among the most

modern afloat," says Browne. "In *Northern Star* there are eighteen ovens, four grill-tables, four fish-fryers. Then there are the bakers' ovens and the steamers. Everything has to be carefully timed to serve anything between five and six hundred meals in half an hour at each sitting. A sitting takes an hour, including the time for the stewards to re-lay the tables."

Browne is under no illusions about occasional complaints by passengers.

"It's their privilege, as it is in any ship, and it would be strange if they didn't have the odd grumble at times," says Browne. "But we have our problems."

One of these is that few men today take up life at sea as caterers or stewards for any length of time. Cooks usually stay for three or four voyages and then go ashore to hotels, the butchers for about four voyages; their standard is good, but change of staff is constant.

A bigger problem is to get good stewards as waiters, the catering officer's fourth department—the other two are barkeepers and cabin stewards.

"Every time we leave Southampton we have many new waiters. Sometimes we have to take any we can get, and their standard varies with the time of the year. In summer, when there is a demand in holiday camps and holiday resorts, there are few who want to come to sea for seventy-six days. During the autumn and winter, when there are not so many jobs ashore, it is an easier problem.

"There are usually a number of youngsters around the twenty mark who go to sea for a year or two to have a look around the world. Most of them are pretty raw. Some have been to schools for waiters, but the course only lasts a fortnight, and although they may get a certificate of efficiency some of them may never make waiters as long as they live."

The search for good waiters is common to all British

shipping lines—and foreign ones, too, for that matter, and seems likely to continue. When they go aboard *Southern Cross* and *Northern Star* they are briefed on their job, and told to ask if they want advice.

"We do our best to train them," says Browne. "They improve as the voyage goes on. But we can only do a certain amount, and in the main—well, we have to leave it to the passengers to train them. If a table gets a dud waiter the passengers soon let him know about it—and us, too. The different standards of waiters is something that is rather difficult to explain to passengers. They pay their fares, they come aboard expecting good service, and for the first week or so it may be uncertain according to the intelligence shown by the man learning his job. Towards the end of the voyage they are becoming really efficient."

Discipline has to be strict, for timetables are rigid in the restaurants. A first breach is met with a warning; a second means that the offender will be taken before the captain and have his pay deducted according to his offence. Desertions do occur.

Normally deserters go ashore at a port and just don't return before the ship sails. A rather more novel and enterprising leave-taking of *Northern Star* was thought out by two young stewards while the ship was anchored three-quarters of a mile off Rarotonga, the "pearl of the Pacific". They built themselves a raft with empty oil-drums and some planks and followed it over the stern while the passengers were enjoying a concert given by a party of Rarotongans.

Unusually for deserters, they left this letter for Captain Edmeads:

DEAR SIR,

Re absence from duty. We regret the above and the inconvenience which may result from same. However, we would advise that upon due reflection we decided to leave the ship and swim ashore at Rarotonga. At this juncture we would hasten to assure you that we are quite competent swimmers and, consequently, by the time this letter comes to hand you may rest assured that we are ashore. Further to the above we would respectfully advise that it is not our intention to return to your vessel and would, therefore, request you do not pursue this matter any further.

Whatever Captain Edmeads may have thought of their enterprise and consideration in writing the letter, his duty was clear. He informed the Rarotongan authorities by radio telephone that the population of their island had increased by two stewards. From Rarotonga the deserters were sent to New Zealand, and then back to England.

"We lost fourteen stewards one voyage," says Browne. "Two went off at Las Palmas, two at Durban, four at Melbourne, six in Wellington. They all had to be rounded up and sent home. Usually we know over the ship's grapevine who is going to desert.

"Fortunately there is another side to the coin. Many stewards look for promotion, and those who do are a steady lot and do a good job."

Other preoccupations of catering officers include losses through breakages and souvenir-hunting. Due to bad weather or accidents or carelessness an average of 3000 plates, 2000 cups, and 10,000 glasses litter the ocean-bed in the wake of *Northern Star* every voyage. About 250 ashtrays disappear during a round voyage, and a number of fruit knives and forks. All have the Shaw Savill crest; more might be taken if they did not.

Laundry is another big item. Nearly a quarter of a million 'pieces' are laundered during each round voyage of *Northern Star*—waiters' cloths, bedroom towels, sheets, pillow-slips, table-napkins. It was suggested that paper table-napkins should be used, but it was found that storage space would be too great, as about half a million would be needed for a round voyage.

If Browne often has a thoughtful look in his eyes it is because he is probably the one man in the ship with a double set of problems—those of the passengers and those of the stewards, whose ideas about service may occasionally conflict.

"We do what we can, and on the whole things go remarkably well," he says.

CHAPTER THIRTEEN

Doctors at Sea

THE nursing sister was puzzled. For the second successive morning she had found that two of the seven beds in the neat, compact women's ward of *Northern Star*'s hospital had obviously been slept in. But no patients had been admitted, and the ward had been empty when she made a cursory check the previous nights. Were stowaways dossing down while nobody was about? Or had two women been taken ill? She reported her discovery and her queries to the ship's surgeon. He was puzzled, too.

That day the usual number of passengers came to the surgery as out-patients, but no women required treatment that would mean being confined to the ward, which remained empty. Just in case the nocturnal visitors returned, the surgeon decided to make an early-morning call. He set his alarm for 3 A.M., when he put on his dressing-gown and set off on what he hoped would be a brief and uneventful inspection.

He switched on the lights in the ward—and saw two beds occupied, grey heads snuggled down under the pink sheets and blankets. Gently, he shook the shoulders of the sleepers, and a moment later was confronted by two very irate elderly women. How dare he wake them? So he was the ship's surgeon? Then he must know they had a perfect right to be in the ward. They were feeling unwell.

"If you are not well, then you should come along

to see me during surgery hours, or send for me to come to see you," said the doctor.

"Young man," one of the women replied, "I have my own doctor in England. He has looked after me for years, and knows all about the turns I have. Before I came aboard he wrote and told me that if ever I felt unwell I must go to hospital. My friend and I have both been poorly, so we did what my doctor told me and have come here. Now go away and leave us alone."

They were left—until morning, when they were told, politely but firmly, that they would be admitted into the ward if they were seriously ill, but not otherwise. Neither was at all ill, but they were not particularly convinced.

They were among the more unusual of the patients in the two ships, where it is normally found that about 1 per cent of the passengers and something like 5 per cent of the crews see the doctors and their staffs every day. They have the normal run-of-the-mill ailments dealt with by any general practitioner ashore; occasionally there are serious cases and accidents, and, more rarely still, calls from other ships.

Both *Southern Cross* and *Northern Star* have modern, well-equipped hospitals designed by the company's medical adviser, staffed by a senior and assistant surgeon, two nursing sisters, and two hospital stewards.

The majority of the passengers probably never see the hospitals—unless they have some professional or personal interest—but, in addition to those who may be ill when they come aboard or are ill during the voyage, there are usually a small number who become well known to the doctors.

Some do their best to have meals served in their cabins on the pretext of illness, but this is a request granted only in genuine cases. There are usually, it

seems, a few people on every voyage—mainly women—
who are determined to have some notice taken of them.
This is a form of psychosis, and, according to the
doctors, its degree differs in *Southern Cross* and
Northern Star.

Both doctors are experienced. In *Southern Cross* is
a man who was brought up and educated in Dublin,
qualifying at the Royal College of Surgeons and
Physicians in October 1944. After a period in the
general hospital at Weston-super-Mare, he was in
general practice for the better part of a year before
volunteering to join the 112th Light Anti-aircraft
Regiment as medical officer. He first went to sea as
senior medical officer in the troopship *Empress of
Australia*. Liking the life, he joined the Bibby Line,
and then Shaw Savill, and was appointed to *Southern
Cross* during 1960.

The doctor in *Northern Star* served with the Royal
Air Force as a bomber pilot during the War, and
qualified at St Bartholomew's Hospital in 1957. After
working as a house surgeon in South London and
Amersham and being medical adviser to a film
company while Ingrid Bergman was making *The Inn
of the Sixth Happiness*, he went to North Wales before
becoming surgical registrar to a hospital in Bucking-
hamshire. This was followed by a year of pathology in
London, where he did just on one thousand post-
mortems, and two and a half years in general practice
in Bermondsey, until slum clearance reduced the
patients by more than half. Uncertain of his next move,
he saw an advertisement in the *Medical Journal* for
a medical officer in *Northern Star*, and joined her for
her second voyage.

"I have found that a doctor has to be much more
tolerant in a ship than in a practice ashore," says
Northern Star's doctor. "Immediately some women see

you in uniform they feel you are somebody they can attack. Occasionally they come to the surgery, plant themselves in a chair, and refuse to leave until their demands are met. There are several types . . . those who say they have travelled a lot—always first-class, of course—and claim they are entitled to the best attention. They get it anyway, because there are no classes in a one-class ship. Some want their breakfast in bed because they are used to having it there, and expect a medical certificate to take to the catering officer. Others want to sleep in the wards; others sometimes attempt to carry their mattresses up on deck and to sleep there—why, I don't know, in an air-conditioned ship.

"Some will complain about their cabins or the steward at their table in the restaurant or the people at their table.

"I think a thesis could probably be written on psychosis in ships, and the effect on certain types of people of a feeling of being confined."

The doctor in *Southern Cross*, however, is inclined to discount this idea.

"We get complaints, of course," he says. "In a troopship there were usually complaints while we were in the tropics. In *Southern Cross* we sometimes get complaints about the air-conditioning. Some people say it gives them colds and coughs. The point is, of course, they don't appreciate—particularly in the tropics—that it is much cooler in their cabins and the restaurants and the cinema lounge, and they don't put on extra clothing like a pullover or a light jacket for a little while after they come in from the heat.

"You will usually get on most voyages one person who is an arch-complainer, another who is a crashing bore, and another who is just about a dypsomaniac. We accept this as a matter of course. It's the same in most ships."

The two doctors also have opposite opinions about how doctors ashore regard ships' doctors. One believes that there is tendency to suggest that ships' doctors personally use alcohol and spirits for purposes that don't come under the classification of 'medicinal'. Sometimes passengers have letters from their own doctors giving their brief case-history, but they have been accompanied by a warning not to worry the ship's doctor except in emergency, because the treatment they receive may not be of a high standard.

"This really disappoints me," said one of the doctors. "I've had patients in the ship who have suffered and been in pain because of letters like this. They've been amazed when they've discovered the excellent equipment we have, and to find that we are just as competent to treat them as anybody else. It can be irritating in other ways. I like an odd drink and to be sociable of an evening in the Tavern or the lounges. But even if I'm drinking plain soda-water somebody will suggest that it's neat gin. Then I insist that they taste it."

The other doctor does not agree about the opinions held ashore of ships' doctors.

"I've never experienced it," he says. "Nor have I had cases of patients not coming to me because of anything their own doctors may have said."

Occasionally during voyages the ship may be blamed for an 'illness'. Some passengers may hear in the launderette or the ironing-room that there is a cold or a certain kind of pain "going round the ship".

They go to the doctor and say, "I've got what everybody else has got."

When asked just what it is that everybody else has, they say, "Well, it's this pain in the chest" or whatever else 'it' is. They are surprised when they are told they are the first to report it.

Serious cases do occur from time to time. A steward in *Southern Cross* was badly beaten up while returning to the ship in Cape Town. His head was cut and his eyes blacked. He was making good progress after two days in hospital, but nine days later—after Las Palmas had been left behind—he appeared to be semi-comatose. Further examinations showed that he was suffering from a sub-dural haemorrhage, caused by his head injuries. The ship's doctor, with a surgeon experienced in neuro-surgery, a passenger, operated and spent nearly four hours drilling two small holes into the skull to remove a blood clot. The steward was flown home from Lisbon, and made a complete recovery.

Operations for appendicitis have been taken as a matter of course, but one grumbling appendix and a case of peritonitis caused some concern in *Northern Star*.

The grumbling appendix was in the *San Fernando*, a Shell oil-tanker en route for Tokyo from Panama, and her captain sent out a message asking for advice and help. *Northern Star* was about 250 miles north-west of Tahiti and the *San Fernando* forty hours' steaming away. Edmeads changed course, and while the two ships were nosing towards one another the doctor sent a number of radio messages to the tanker's captain. From the answers to his questions he diagnosed appendicitis, and directed treatment with chloromycetin and penicillin.

The ships hove-to a mile apart, and the doctor was rowed in a lifeboat through a rough sea to the tanker, where he decided that the patient should be brought back to *Northern Star*. There it was found that the appendix had responded to the drugs and subsided, and an immediate operation was unnecessary. It was performed after the patient arrived in England.

"What impressed me," said *Northern Star*'s doctor, "was the ability and the intelligence of the captain of the *San Fernando*. He told me by radio everything I wanted to know, and it meant that the treatment I prescribed was successful. I wrote a letter of appreciation to Shell."

The peritonitis case developed suddenly when *Northern Star* was nearing Southampton. A woman required major surgery, for a leak from the bowel occurred, and the doctor preferred that the operation should be in a hospital ashore. Edmeads rang for full speed and was on the bridge for forty-eight hours. *Northern Star* docked four hours ahead of schedule, the patient was on the operating-table within the hour, and in a short time was making a normal recovery.

"It was a big responsibility for the captain," the doctor said. "He could have told me to operate. But I satisfied him that no harm could come to the patient before we could get her ashore."

Not all patients are put ashore. In Durban a woman beginning her voyage slipped in the customs shed, fracturing and dislocating an elbow. The doctor was summoned and, at the same time, an ambulance sent for. The patient was upset, as well as being in pain.

"I've waited three months for this trip," she said. "Now I'll have to go to hospital and miss it."

"We have a hospital in the ship, madam," said the doctor. "If you like to come aboard we can look after you. There is no need for you to miss your holiday."

When she went ashore at Fremantle the fracture was knitting nicely.

Some patients are ungrateful. A cook got drunk in Sydney, fell into the harbour, and was hauled aboard unconscious. He seemed, in fact, to be dead; he was not breathing. *Northern Star*'s doctor had him suspended by his feet and gave him a sharp blow on the back. The cook vomited and began to gasp. A few minutes later he was in hospital, where air was pumped into his lungs for four hours. The remainder of the night was spent patching him up, for his other injuries included a fractured skull. Ten days later he was discharged from hospital—and appeared at a logging session before the captain. He was furious at being docked a week's pay.

"You're lucky to be alive and able to lose your pay," said the doctor.

The cook was unconvinced.

One patient who was grateful was John Bridgman, aged twenty-one, an assistant steward in *Northern Star*. While the ship was off Tahiti early in October 1964 he dived into the swimming-pool from a height of twenty feet.

"I bumped my head on the bottom, but it didn't hurt much. I swam around for a bit, and dived in again before going to bed. The next thing I knew was when I woke up to find that I'd had an operation and that the doctor had saved my life," he said.

Bridgman had, in fact, become unconscious in bed, for he had bumped his skull so severely on the tiled floor of the pool that a blood clot formed, causing severe brain compression. The doctor was called when Bridgman could not be roused.

Once he had made his diagnosis the doctor realized that Bridgman's life could be saved only by the removal of the blood clot, and that this necessitated a major operation.

"It was difficult and tricky, and I knew before I started that I needed two things—the luck to find the clot and the guts to break in and disperse it. For two hours I studied a book on brain surgery and I knew it by heart when I went into the theatre," he said.

He had, of course, full equipment for the operation,

but there were two instruments he decided that would be useful, one as a stand-by—an electric drill and a chisel ground to a razor-sharp edge—and these were provided by the chief electrician and the chief engineer.

The operation lasted five and a half hours. The doctor bored four holes with the drill in Bridgman's skull, but did not find the blood clot. He tapped it at the fifth attempt. It was thirty hours after Bridgman was wheeled from the theatre to a bed in the small ward before he woke up to find his head swathed in bandages and a smiling—and relieved—doctor looking down at him. He was able to walk ashore at Southampton and to travel to his home at Amesbury, in Wiltshire.

"I like the life at sea," said the *Star*'s doctor when talking about his job. "I like having my own hospital. I like looking after a patient throughout the whole illness. Human nature is just as interesting in a ship as in a general practice—in fact, rather more interesting, for you certainly discover some new facets to it."

CHAPTER FOURTEEN

"You need Stamina"

THERE may be a trend away from the sea by men—but women are queueing up to be a hostess, a purserette, or a nursing sister. Anything up to eighteen months is a fairly normal period for them to wait before they can sign on in *Southern Cross* or *Northern Star*. They have to be in their mid-twenties at least, fully qualified and experienced, mature in outlook, and used to dealing with people *en masse*.

Their motives are the normal ones—a desire to travel, to see the world, get away from home, to change jobs and routine, and possibly find a husband. It is a romantic potential, but the work is no sinecure, hours are often long—particularly before sailing and arriving—and shore leave at the various ports not automatic. They all seem to enjoy it.

The idea of having a hostess aboard was an innovation for the maiden voyage of *Northern Star*. There was a rather tentative approach to it in the ship, so the purser was given discretion to decide at Las Palmas as to whether or not she should continue the voyage or return home from there.

This, at any rate, was the impression of Mrs Doreen Crawley, *Northern Star*'s first hostess, who was able to prove that there was a job to be done. Just what it was she was not quite sure, for during the trials and the shake-down cruises she was often told to make herself scarce. But she did not return home from Las Palmas.

Although she had been a passenger in various ships of other lines Mrs Crawley admitted that as a house-wife and former WAAF officer she knew relatively little about ships; yet she was accustomed to dealing with people.

She was born in Callao, from where the Kon-Tiki raft set off from Peru for its drift across the Pacific. Her father was a master mariner and marine super-intendent at Talara, and returned to England with his wife and daughter when Doreen was eight. In March 1941 she joined the WAAF as an A.C.2 (plotter), and was sent to Jesus College, Cambridge, to take a course in psychology prior to being posted to a team of four pre-selection personnel interviewers whose job was to estimate whether pilots should fly fighter or bomber aircraft or, perhaps, be grounded. She was com-missioned as assistant section officer in June the following year. She married in January 1948, and resigned her commission a few months later.

Mrs Crawley was first attracted to the idea of being a social hostess when she read an advertisement by Shaw Savill inviting applications. Her brief was defined as assisting elderly women and women travel-ling alone to enjoy life at sea by encouraging them to take part in the ship's social activities; and to be responsible to the purser. At the end of two voyages she had proved the value of a social hostess aboard, and, after a brief break ashore, transferred from *Northern Star* to *Southern Cross*.

Mrs Crawley was succeeded in *Northern Star* by Miss Jeanne Pratt, whose father worked in Shaw Savill's head office until retiring, and whose mother's family had bred sailors since the days of Drake. By the time she was eight Jeanne announced that at some time in the indefinite future she would go to Norway and take her master's certificate. Even though Reigate, in the heart of Surrey, was the nearest she could get to the sea, she made herself a cabin in the garage loft, furnished it with an uncle's old sea-chest, spent hours drawing and painting sailing-ships, and put up a notice to indicate whether "the captain" was in or out. She did, however, go aboard the *Pamir* and, when she was eleven, *Dominion Monarch*, where, with a number of small boys, she clambered up a mast.

It was several years later before she saw *Dominion Monarch* again, and this time she went to sea in her as a purserette. She was in *Northern Star* for the maiden voyage. From purserette to hostess was a short step.

Being at sea gave her the opportunity of realizing at least part of her childhood ambition: in Wellington, a far cry from Norway, she received her certificate endorsing her qualification to command a lifeboat powered by engine, sail, or oars. The test was practical and oral. First she had to take charge of a lifeboat, direct the crew while rescuing an imaginary body in the sea, and return to the ship. Then she had to say how she would bring a lifeboat ashore in heavy surf.

Unlike the officers, the hostess in *Southern Cross* and *Northern Star* does not wear uniform; she is identified by a coloured badge bearing the Line's crest and the word "hostess". Her success depends on personality, a definition which, vague as it may be, conveys so many intangibles—charm, tact, tolerance, empathy, sympathy, firmness, shrewdness.

Like the officers, she has a routine, which includes frequent consultation with the purser and the catering officer on programmes and personalities. She boards the ship at Southampton the day before sailing, and is in the main foyer while passengers embark, noting, observing, and already answering questions. By the time the Needles are disappearing below the horizon she has a list of those she will seek out to help them settle down and become accustomed to the ship.

Usually there are a few elderly women who may be seasick or out of sorts whom she will visit in their cabins shortly after eight each morning. Later she will go to the main deck foyer while the tables in the restaurants are filling for the second breakfast sitting; the remainder of the morning until noon she will divide her time between the lounges, meeting people and helping them to mix. During the afternoon there may be gatherings to arrange and supervise—the start of the contract-bridge and chess circles, a lecture, a showing of camera slides or ciné-films, or 'hen parties', when women with similar interests such as nursing or women's guilds gather together. A popular weekly session is "Woman's Hour", when speakers from among the passengers are invited to talk on any subject of their own choosing, answer questions, and encourage discussion.

The hostess attends the captain's cocktail parties, and before the evening is ended will call at the hospital to talk with patients and the medical staff. After dinner she will keep an eye open for elderly people who may seem to need encouragement to take part in bingo sessions or race meetings, or perhaps just to watch the dancers.

It all means hours of talking, giving information about the ship and its activities and the tours that may be made at the next port, offering personal advice or listening to confidences. Some of the elderly women may be at sea for the first time, travelling to see relatives or to a new home, and may be worried, lonely, or uncertain; they appreciate a heart-to-heart talk and being introduced to somebody who may be in exactly the same situation. There may be diabetics aboard: they are taken to the catering officer and a special diet arranged. There may be some who arrive with a chip on their shoulder, an expression of their own personal problems which they have been unable to cope with, and who consciously or unconsciously want to draw attention to themselves; or they may develop a chip because they have been unable to settle down on board. There may be others who are shy and withdrawn and who may not have met anybody with whom they feel they can make friends. The hostess does her best to help them all. It is also part of her work to be a Press liaison officer in port, and to assist reporters to interview passengers.

It is not an easy job, nor is it one that can be done for a few hours and forgotten. It is important as a contribution to a contented atmosphere in the ship and part of the grapevine that informs the captain, the purser, the catering officer, and the doctor of the passengers' attitude to the ship and to one another.

The purserette's work can be described as mainly secretarial, but with social obligations. There is a considerable amount of typing of documents needed at ports, of programmes, of lists, of overtime sheets, of letters. On the social side she helps with the crossword puzzle and book-title competitions, with bingo sessions, race meetings, preparing and wrapping prizes for presentation by the captain, and, in *Northern Star*, typing certificates for the ceremony of crossing the equator. The hours are long, particularly before, during, and immediately after the ship's stay in port. She is often on duty in the purser's office answering inquiries, or in the main foyer when passengers are embarking.

In *Northern Star* Miss Shirley Ravenscroft succeeded Miss Jeanne Pratt as purserette. Unlike Mrs Crawley and Miss Pratt, her family had no connections with the sea. After education at Pinner, in Middlesex, she did a secretarial course and changed jobs several times. A

trip to Continental ports in the *Port Hobart* prompted
the idea of becoming a purserette. When she saw a
photograph of a girl in naval uniform enjoying
Christmas at Las Palmas aboard the *Cape Town Castle*
she applied to the Union Castle Line, and was invited
for an interview.

"I had the necessary qualifications," she says. "I
was the right age—over twenty-three—I had several
G.C.E. passes, I had been trained by a recognized
London secretarial college, and I had experience of
wage accounts."

Her first job was in *Carnarvon Castle*, and for a
period she was in *Durban Castle*, plying along the
east coast of Africa. After a long leave ashore she
became a hotel receptionist, but she missed the life at
sea. Attracted by the idea of sailing round the world,
she applied to Shaw Savill, working in London in a
solicitor's office while on the waiting-list.

Miss Mary Fowler, purserette in *Southern Cross*, an
experienced secretary, had her education at Coulsdon,
in Surrey, worked in a stockbroker's office, and then
with an oil firm, going to sea in cargo-ships for her
holidays and sailing to Norway, the Mediterranean,
Trinidad, and South America. This gave her the idea
of working at sea, and she was on the Shaw Savill
waiting-list for a year and a half.

Of the nursing sisters, Miss Margaret Davies is the
doyen of the Line. She has been at sea for over sixteen
years, many of them in *Dominion Monarch*, and was
transferred from *Northern Star* to *Southern Cross* early
in 1964. She did her training at the Middlesex Hospital.
Miss Anne Parker, who also trained there, joined her
in *Northern Star* for the maiden voyage. Others in
Southern Cross have been Miss Jocelyn Swears, a New
Zealander trained at New Plymouth, who was second
staff nurse for three years at the East Grinstead

Hospital in Sussex, where she saw the New Zealand plastic surgeon, the late Sir Archibald McIndoe, at work; and Miss Judith Knill Jones, trained at Addenbrooke's Hospital, Cambridge, who was in the casualty department at the Sutton and Cheam General Hospital, Surrey.

All welcome the change from the routine of a big hospital "with its rules and red tape", and like being expected to use their initiative while caring for passengers of all ages, "from babies to elderly ladies". They start at 7.30 A.M. on rounds of cabins with the doctors, and attend morning and evening surgeries. They find they "more or less run a casualty station as well as a hospital". One nursing sister is always 'on call' for twenty-four hours, and she may deal with anything from a common cold to a vaccination or assist in the theatre during a major operation.

The purserettes, the nursing sisters, and the children's hostesses have their cabins together aft— the hostesses have passenger cabins—and share the deck officers' smoke-room; they also share the officers' deck for sun-bathing.

"The days and weeks fly by," says Shirley Ravenscroft. "The whole of your life is organized, and there's not much time to think far beyond what you are doing at the moment and what comes immediately after it. You're always busy, and when you're not working there's always somebody to talk to. The officers usually take turns in giving pre-dinner cocktail parties in their day cabins—more often than not it's a case of standing-room only—we join in the social life of the ship and go to the dances and other entertainments, and we usually get some time off ashore in the ports. In many ways we live in a closed community—but it's an interesting life."

"You need stamina," says Mary Fowler, "but only sheer tiredness would drive me ashore."

CHAPTER FIFTEEN

Twopence Ha'penny a Mile

AROUND the world in eighty days" might be the theme song of *Southern Cross* and *Northern Star* as their propellers churn evanescent lace patterns in the great oceans of the world and their sterns dip a never-ceasing farewell to the horizon. With their strict punctuality they clip four days off Jules Verne's journey.

Departure from Southampton is normally at three o'clock in the afternoon. Passengers may drive to the dock by car or taxi or, according to their position in the alphabetical list, catch one of two trains from Waterloo Station. The first leaves at 9.15 A.M., the second less than an hour later, when London commuters on their way to work cast wistful glances at gaily coloured luggage-labels, particularly if the weather is grey and dull. As they queue at the ticket-barrier the passengers for the most part look thoughtful, the main suggestion of excitement coming from children. The run to Southampton takes about an hour and forty minutes, give or take five or ten minutes, much of it through pleasant, placid countryside, and the train pulls up alongside a customs shed next to the ship.

Going through customs is a jostling formality, and includes the presentation of a boarding-card. In the main foyer stewards hover to take suitcases and lead the way to cabins, and the hostess, a purserette, and one or two other officers are there to help with directions. Luncheon is more or less at leisure. Cards notifying future table-placings and sittings are in every cabin, so that passengers know where to take their places at dinner and, unless they request to change, for the remainder of their voyage.

As sailing-time approaches and unpacking has been completed and the lounges explored, there is a drift to the rails on the decks looking down on the wharf and customs shed, which has a touch of colour added by the Union Jack and the Shaw Savill House Flag. The last of the visitors leave, tug-lines are looped on, ropes cast off, the gangways separate from the ship, and loudspeakers deliver *A Life on the Ocean Wave*. There is a buzz of "She's moving", and farewell waves from ship and wharf become more vigorous. Here and there a moist eye is dabbed. Parting is not always sweet sorrow. Now the tugs strain like bull mastiffs, greeny water swirls to muddiness, seagulls squawk like lost souls. The music stops. An almost eerie silence settles over the ship as the distance from the wharf increases. Gradually the ear becomes accustomed to a steady pulsing—the note of the engines as they turn the propellers which begin to crochet the start of the trail of watery lace that will bubble and froth over more than 27,000 miles before Southampton is seen again. The voyage has begun. England will soon be just a memory.

Passengers have already found in their cabins a letter from the captain bidding them welcome and wishing them an enjoyable voyage. As the days tick by they will receive regular delivery of information about entertainments and sports, and the news bulletin. A day or two before arriving at the next port there will also be a brochure giving a potted history of the country and the city or town that lies ahead, illustrated by photographs and maps. The first on the east-about voyage is entitled "Las Palmas, Canary Islands".

It says that the word "Canary" dates from the days of the Romans, who found *canaria*—dogs of great size—in the archipelago, that the Spaniards began building Las Palmas, the capital of Grand Canary, in 1478, and settled in as conquerors after killing off or inter-marrying with the aborigine Guanches. Today it is a popular holiday resort, with a pleasantly unvaried climate, and a population of about 178,000. The island is stippled with extinct volcanoes, and its main income is from the export of bananas, potatoes, and tomatoes, and the advantages of Las Palmas being a free port.

It has been a criticism of some lines that many passengers see more of a port from a brochure than by going ashore, since ships arrive at night and sail at daylight. This does not apply to *Southern Cross* and *Northern Star*, whose schedules ensure that they tie up in the early morning.

Thus arrival at Las Palmas is at 7 A.M., and departure eleven hours later, ample time for coach tours or visits to the city by taxi and a sampling of Spanish atmosphere. It is equally pleasant to drive inland for a variety of views as it is to bathe in a sea that is gratifyingly warm after some of the cooler dips round the English coasts; the sun is inclined to burn rather than to tan. There seem to be mixed opinions about the business acumen of both taxi-drivers and the vendors allowed on board to offer a wide range of wares. One is that as bargaining appears to be a national pastime, any prices mentioned should be halved and bidding begun on that basis. Whatever their experiences, passengers are usually content when the ship draws away from the wharf and the town's rather yellowy-boxy buildings gradually disappear from sight.

Arrival at Cape Town, dominated by the magnificent

mass of Table Mountain, is much more of an event, particularly for homecoming South Africans, deeply proud of their country and defensive or non-committal about its politics and apartheid. Many are up on the observation deck before dawn while the lights of the city are still glinting like yellow gems. Table Mountain is first seen as a black hump against the sky, dark, brooding, its bulk intensified as the sky blushes pink and maroon before sunrise. The ship slides silently nearer, black becomes grey, and gradually the flat top of the mountain and Lion's Head and Devil's Peak are defined. Sunrise can be magnificent. The outline of the mountain and the distant ranges grows sharper, and suddenly, like an electric bulb switched on, the tip of old Phoebus appears, a small pinpoint of light that grows to a round, blazing ball.

Ship routine continues until breakfast, which is followed by an orderly scramble for mail, farewells to South African friends before they go through customs, and a steady streaming down the gangways for coach tours or carefree wandering. Some people may be going on to Durban by road or air. If it is a clear and relatively windless day—and Cape Town is no stranger to wind—others will take taxi or bus to the cable-car and the steep haul to the top of Table Mountain and the magnificent view so beloved by General Smuts, that great South African statesman who scorned the ride and preferred to walk.

To see from 3000 feet the nestling city, the peaks, the bays, the distant ranges, and sea and sky merging into the blue distance is to experience "beauty in her naked blaze". Descent is an anticlimax. But there is much to enjoy.

The drive round Chapman's Peak is reminiscent of the Spanish coast; and to visit, for instance, Groot Constantia, an old wine farm a dozen miles or so from the city and first settled in 1691, is to dip into the roots of South African history and its proud families, including the Cloetes. Those who hire cars will find excellent roads, and those who prefer to shop need not wander from Adderley Street. The day passes too quickly, and may be completed by a "night lights" tour. By eight o'clock next morning the ship is moving on to Durban, twenty-four hours after tying up.

Durban is South Africa's third largest city, a holiday centre as well as a main port and centre of industry. Arrival is at 8.30 A.M., and the routine is much the same as at Cape Town. There is a six-hour drive to the native markets, the Valley of One Thousand Hills, and a Zulu kraal. Bargaining in the Indian market has a certain humour unknown in Las Palmas, and a ride in a rickshaw drawn by an ornamental Zulu has more leisure and character than a sprint by taxi. The heights of Berea, the city gardens, and the beaches make many wistful. Passengers leave with many memories, including, probably, Zulu dancing or perhaps just lazing aboard, treating the ship as a floating hotel, and contemplating the city's lights after sunset. By the first breakfast sitting next morning Durban is already two hours behind, and many South Africans are settling down, too, for the ten-day run 4334 miles across the Indian Ocean to Fremantle and Perth, capital of Western Australia and named after the capital city of ancient Scotland.

Now it is the returning Australians who are exuberant at the first sight of their own country, and, while Fremantle is an efficient port, it is Perth, twelve miles away on the northern bank of the Swan river, that has a charm few ever forget. The Swan river, Mount Eliza, the thousand acres of King's Park, and the view of the Darling Range, seen in a pale purple haze, are among the magnets that make passengers wish they were staying longer than nine hours. There is surf-bathing on great rollers lapping in from miles of ocean; and for golfers who wish to stretch their legs on turf after days of plodding round wooden decks there are blue-gum sheltered links where the kookaburra's raucous laugh echoes muttering after a topped drive or missed putt.

With Fremantle behind, the Great Australian Bight lies ahead, and as the ship nods on to Melbourne the coastline of Victoria is to port, miles of surf beating against cliffs, sandy islands, and inlets, and mountains rising loftily in the distance. For many passengers it will be journey's end at Melbourne, capital of Victoria, second largest city in Australia, and seventh city of the British Commonwealth. Some will travel overland to Sydney; others make full use of the twenty-nine hours—from 4 P.M. to 9 P.M. the following day—and, while sampling the city, also have their first sight of koalas, lyre birds, kangaroos, wallabies, and the platypus. Melbourne has a reputation for uncertain climate—"you can have all the seasons of the year in one day"—but whatever the weather there is plenty to see and do.

It is a new experience for people from Britain and South Africa to drive to the Dandenong Ranges through miles of virgin bush and towering trees. Some will seek Captain Cook's cottage in the Fitzroy Gardens, others go to St Kilda and Brighton beaches, others to Sir Colin Mackenzie's wild-life sanctuary. Shopping is no problem, but the brochure has a reminder that Australians, friendly and forthright, also have among them certain specious individuals known the world over as 'con men'. "Passengers are warned", says the brochure, "against entering into any arrangements with persons purporting to be agents for money-changing firms or banks, or itinerant pedlars of merchandise."

By the time the ship reaches Sydney the half-way mark in the round voyage has arrived, and, as she enters the harbour, one of the best moments of all seventy-six days. Few passengers will now be prepared to dispute with Australians the beauty of "our 'arbour" or the grandeur of "our bridge", or to refuse an opportunity to sail round the harbour and under the bridge, or to neglect strolling across the great structure —which has its miniature twin at Newcastle-on-Tyne, where it was designed and where *Northern Star* was built.

With over two million people and the capital of New South Wales, Sydney is the biggest city visited during the entire voyage, and it has everything a big city has to offer—plus. There are so many 'pluses'— its buildings, the zoological gardens at Taronga Park, the royal flush of beaches at Bondi, Manly, Coogee, Cronulla, and Palm Beach; its racecourse, its cricket-grounds, its night-clubs. There are so many tours. One of the most popular is to Bulli Pass, the Sublime Point, and back through Lady Carrington Drive in the national park, claimed as the best of its kind in Australia. Another is to the Blue Mountains and Katoomba and Leura, over 3000 feet above sea-level, and to the Jenolan Caves.

The ship stays forty-seven hours in Sydney, and when she leaves there have been many farewells as well as welcomes, for there is a big turn-over of passengers. Coloured paper streamers link her briefly to the wharf before she sails, and as she moves out sedately to the Sydney Heads and the swell of the Tasman Sea the harbour is often alive with yachts and cheerful waving.

"Windy Wellington" lies ahead, capital of New Zealand, where over 158,000 of the country's 2½ million people live, and are as proud of its harbour

as the Aussies are of Sydney's. At first sight it seems
to be built on hills, and though Kelburn—400 feet up
by cable-car—is a mild hump compared with Table
Mountain, it has an outstanding panoramic view of the
city, the harbour, and the distant Tararua Mountains
and the flat expanse of Lower Hutt. The ship stays for
two and a half days, there is another big turnover of
passengers, and many who embarked at Southampton,
except the round-voyagers, leave her. Wellington is the
biggest 'turn-round' port, all cabins are cleaned and
turned out, the galley staff has some rest, and, as at
Sydney, the bulk of fresh stores is taken aboard.

If the ship is also calling at Auckland many round-
voyagers, and South Africans and Australians, may
travel overland, visiting *en route* Rotorua, where Maori
guides show them spouting geysers and boiling mud-
pools, and the glow-worm caves at Waitomo. As an
alternative they may fly to South Island and perhaps
penetrate as deeply as Milford Sound before catching
up with the ship at Auckland.

Wellington and its windiness is not without its
hazards, as Captain Edmeads has never forgotten. It
was there that *Northern Star* had a repetition of her
experience when leaving the Tyne. Normally the
prevailing winds at Wellington blow either up or down
the wharves, but on one occasion when *Northern Star*
was moving slowly away a strong wind changed
direction briefly, but of sufficient duration to push the
ship round 45 degrees. Time, distance, and speed were
against her, and she struck the ends of Glasgow Wharf
and Pipitea Wharf a glancing blow, damaging them
and herself—fortunately above the water-line.

Auckland is a bigger city than Wellington, with a
population of over 499,700, and her harbour and her
bridge are rivals to Sydney's. From Mount Eden, an
extinct volcano 600 feet above sea-level, the view

competes with Kelburn's at Wellington. Yachting is as popular as in South Island and across the Tasman Sea. As the ship leaves New Zealand and begins to nose into the Pacific northwards to Suva, the capital of Fiji, there are many for whom the three days and two nights have been too short, whetting the appetite but not satisfying it. Fishermen regret having had no more than a glance at rainbow trout at Taupo, golfers sigh at leaving behind so many fine courses, and those who like lazing on beaches or just messing about in boats ponder why so many New Zealanders seem intent on sampling Britain and the Continent when they have Nature's finest gifts spread so relatively inexpensively around them.

The weather becomes warmer and more humid as the propellers churn their lacy wake again, and heat is one of the first impressions of Suva—heat and colour and tropical vegetation and the mixture of races, Melanesian, Tongan, and Indian. The Fijian Police band, in native costume, gives a rousing welcome as the ship docks at 8 A.M. The town rises into thickly forested mountains, where a fire seems to burn perpetually, exuding blue, misty smoke. There is much bargaining to be done, for transistors, tape-recorders, cameras, and binoculars. There are several tours and drives to coral reefs and trips in glass-bottomed boats. "And good beer at the Yacht Club", one connoisseur has noted. At 6 P.M., while the Fijian policemen are playing again, the ship leaves promptly to dodge the rhinoceros beetles. If any strayed from the coconut plantations at dusk and settled on the ship they would be carried on to Papeete, and the Tahitians have strict regulations to keep out these voracious insects from their trees.

Even for those who regard Sydney as the plum of the voyage there is a distinctive appeal about Papeete and Tahiti. While the ship is still well out to sea a land breeze redolent of tropical flowers and coconut-oil sharpens enthusiasm for the magnificent panoramic view. Papeete is difficult to approach from a navigational aspect, and if the weather is threatening it has to be by-passed. The channel through the coral reefs to the harbour is narrow, there are no tugs, and only about two ship's lengths of swinging ground. *Northern Star* is the biggest liner to call, and finds leaving even more tricky than arriving.

The hills of Tahiti, shrouded in mist, are reminiscent of the Valley of One Thousand Hills. The waterfront, on the edge of the small town of Papeete, is dominated by the background scenery and tall, slender coconut palms. The wharf swarms with motor scooters which the shapely Tahitian women ride, their long black hair flowing. Leis of frangipani necklace the passengers who relax appreciatively in the warm, heavy-scented air, listen to Tahitian bands, watch the girls dancing the fluid, sinuous hula, and are easily enticed into buying presents in the shops stringing along the waterfront.

The ship stays twenty-three hours, so there is ample time for driving round the island to see where Captain Cook and then the Bounty mutineers landed, and to swim from perfect beaches in clear, warm water; time to dine in the hotels and contemplate the ship, resembling a huge cake lit by candles, and to wander into bars. Some passengers stay up all night, deciding to make up sleep across the final lap of the Pacific to Balboa and Panama. There are many Chinese, the atmosphere is French, and the currency is the colonial Pacific franc. The cold breath of winter never touches the island, fevers are unknown, food and flowers grow in profusion. Nobody forgets Tahiti.

Now the ship sidles up to and crosses the equator on

the longest haul of the voyage—4494 miles, or just
fifty miles further than from Las Palmas to Cape
Town—to reach the heavy humidity of Balboa and the
entrance to the Panama Canal. She arrives at 2 P.M.
and leaves at 6 A.M., opportunity enough to see
something of Balboa and drive into Old Panama and
Panama City, where the main attractions for a night
out are the Latin-American night-clubs, said to rival
those in Paris. Some visitors are depressed by the
extremes of wealth and poverty, luxurious homes and
buildings contrasting sharply with areas of slums and
shanties "like tomato-boxes". Shopping can be expensive, but women with an eye for crocodile-skin
bags and shoes learn that they are genuine and from
the local crocodile 'farms'. The atmosphere, like that
of Las Palmas, is Spanish, and the spoken word is
said to be little different from its Castilian origin.

From Balboa, headquarters of the Panama Canal
Company and the Canal Zone Government, it takes
about seven and a half hours to go through the canal,
through the locks and lake, to Cristobal. Details of
this great engineering work are broadcast by a commentator who boards the ship with the pilot. There is
a stretch of eight miles to the Miraflores Locks,
nearly a mile long and fifty-four feet above sea-level,
and the ship reaches eighty-five feet above sea-level in
the Gatun Lake. An eighteen-hole golf course is on
top of the Gatun Dam, where the locks bring the ship
down again to sea-level and a seven-mile run to
Cristobal. The length of the canal from deep water
in the Pacific to deep water in the Atlantic is just over
fifty miles. Most passengers prefer to take a light
lunch on deck, watch the scenery sliding past, and
listen to facts, figures, and history.

The pilot and the commentator are dropped at
Cristobal, and the ship threads her way between

vessels of all shapes and sizes to Caracas Bay, in Curaçao, where she fills up with fuel-oil and there are five and a half hours in which to see the Dutch town of Willemstad, capital of the island. It is all too short to do more than sample "this jewel in a West Indian setting", where the population of about 130,000 is made up of forty-five different races, but most people make a point of seeing the floating market filled with craft from Venezuela.

The final port of the voyage—unless an alternative route is taken—is Trinidad, about seven miles north of Venezuela. Port of Spain, the capital with 100,000 people, is the main attraction for some; but for others there is more immediate appeal in driving fourteen miles to Maracas Bay and the ideal of a tropical beach, half-mooned, palm-fringed, with warm, creaming surf. Every prospect pleases, except for ubiquitous and hungry dogs. Everywhere on the island there is a lush growth of vegetation, and an abundance of sugar-cane, grapefruit, and bananas. The largest oil refinery and one of the biggest sugar factories in the Commonwealth are in Trinidad—and 114 acres of an asphalt-producing pitch lake. In the city the shops and the night-clubs offer a final fling before the last leg of ocean to Southampton, 3846 miles away. The tinkling thrum of the steel bands and their inverted oil-drums lingers in the memory.

Occasionally *Southern Cross* and *Northern Star* visit Raratonga, Acapulco, the Mexican holiday resort, Miami, and Bermuda, and sometimes Barbados and Lisbon, all of which have their own special appeal, usually under a blazing sun. Once they have been left behind, the greyness of Atlantic skies can be expected—even during the summer—and the air begins to feel cool and crisp after the tropical heat.

As the ships approach England the crew develops

"the channels"—a feeling of restless excitement on nearing home; the passengers, too, are busy planning ahead, the voyage already becoming an enjoyable memory that will live on in camera-slides and films and in one or two friendships. At Southampton there is mail, and customs, and trains to be boarded.

For the round-voyagers it is nearly journey's end; for South Africans, Australians, and New Zealanders the beginning of a different way of life for a limited or indefinite period. Some, too, may be round-voyagers with a week or ten days to spend in Britain or on the Continent before the ship sets off to circle the earth once more.

Of the seventy-six days since she left Southampton ten days eight hours have been spent in thirteen ports. She has covered 27,324 miles at a minimum rate for each passenger of twopence-halfpenny a mile—which is cheaper, for a mile, than any bus or Underground journey in London. And what a journey!

CHAPTER SIXTEEN

"We shall continue..."

A LITTLE more than a year after *Northern Star* sailed on her maiden voyage Lord Sanderson retired as chairman of Shaw Savill Line. A brief announcement was made on October 12th, 1963. He was succeeded by MacConochie and continued as a director. Sir Errington Keville remained deputy chairman—he had been chairman of Furness, Withy since August 1962, and he was also chairman now of the International Chamber of Shipping, and of the Committee of European National Shipowners' Associations.

It was typical of Lord Sanderson, averse to personal publicity of any kind, that the change should be effected quietly and unobtrusively. There were no formalities, no luncheons, no presentations to mark the end of another chapter in the history of the management of the Line, now stretching back for one hundred and five years. He moved to another room on the opposite side of the building in Leadenhall Street, where he was available for consultation and where he worked on his other wide interests, travelling up from Ayot Bury less regularly. He seemed surprised when letters streamed in from friends all over the world.

Something of what he felt for the Line, and what it meant to him, was apparent when he spoke briefly at the annual staff dinner the following May, when MacConochie presided.

"My whole working life has been associated with

this great company," he said, when the applause which greeted him died to silence. "My interests have been those of the company. My joy has been the service of the company. The company today stands very high, and I am proud of such little part as I have been able to play.

"We have," he continued, "a very great company and a very great tradition. We are accepted throughout the country as a company second to none, and ahead of most. Do keep the flag flying. Do keep the standard up. And then, year after year, you will be able to drink the toast of 'The Company' with the utmost pride."

By now a fresh chapter had begun. MacConochie occupied the chairman's room, and Russell, general manager since 1961, sat next door at MacConochie's former table. In their early fifties, they had worked their way up from the lowest rungs of the company's ladder. Both had been juniors, or office-boys; both had succeeded by sheer ability.

Russell started at the age of sixteen in the passenger office of the Aberdeen and Commonwealth Line in Australia House during July 1929, when 27s. 9d. a week was almost a princely salary for a lad of that age. His father was a tally clerk with George Thompson and Co. The family lived in East Ham, and Russell was educated at Wakefield Road Central School.

The beginning of the thirties was a difficult economic period. Three years after he had joined the Aberdeen and Commonwealth Line, Russell found himself out of a job when the Line amalgamated with Shaw Savill. Believing that the Civil Service should offer a more reasonable hope of permanent employment, he sat for an entrance examination, and missed a pass by only four marks. However, it meant that he was free to continue temporary work when his old firm discovered that its retrenchments had been rather too severe.

Just as the chance of four marks decided his career for the remainder of the thirties, so some rather bumpy landings while learning to fly kept him out of the Royal Air Force Volunteer Reserve in the spring of 1938 and influenced his War service. In March 1941 he joined the Royal Navy as a rating. His first ship was the minesweeper H.M.S. *Gossamer*, which sailed with the first Russian convoy—PQ1—to Archangel from Belfast the following September. She was away from Britain until the end of the year, mine-sweeping in the White Sea, and evacuating a Hurricane wing from Murmansk.

By April 1942 Russell was commissioned as a sub-lieutenant, after a course at H.M.S. *King Alfred*, at Hove. He was appointed first officer in the trawler *Avalanche*, attached to the Dover Command, and then her captain when she served in the decoy area of Dover during the invasion in June 1944. In December he recommissioned the trawler *Trondra*, and was in Iceland until the end of the European War. By May 1946 he was back in Shaw Savill's customs and forwarding office.

Early in 1948 he was selected by Keville to be trained for management, an opportunity which he welcomed, and on January 1st, 1951, he was appointed one of three assistant managers. His first visit to Australia and New Zealand was in 1956; the following year he became chairman of the Australian Tonnage Committee. He was appointed a director in June 1958, a manager in January 1959, and general manager in November 1961—three months after his forty-eighth birthday and just over thirty-two years since he had first gone to work in Australia House.

The careers of MacConochie and Russell were typical of the encouragement given by Sanderson and Keville to younger men showing a flair for management. Another of the post-War generation, who was to know *Northern Star* from bow to stern, was R. A. Huskisson.

He joined the Line in September 1947 at twenty-four after six years with the Royal Corps of Signals.

Huskisson's father was general manager and a director of Thomas Cook and Sons, who sent his son to Merchant Taylors' School. There, among other things, Huskisson enjoyed Rugby football and was coached by a former All Black, K. R. J. Saxon. When he left school at eighteen he joined the Royal Corps of Signals in 1941. He was sent to St Edmund Hall, Oxford, for a six months' course, and played in the 'Varsity pack during the 1941-42 Rugby season. He served in France and Belgium, and finished the War as a captain in Air Formation Signals in Berlin; as a major he left the Army in El Ballah, Egypt, in 1947.

Huskisson started with Shaw Savill in the statistical department, working on costings, voyage estimates, and project organization; and he had an influence on a different type of figures when he continued his Rugby football, captain and a front row forward of Old Merchant Taylors' and of Eastern Counties. From the beginning of 1951 until the autumn of 1952 he gained an insight into the Line's business in Australia and New Zealand; the following year he became head of the crew department, responsible for the payment of the seamen's wages, allotments, and welfare.

In 1956, aged thirty-three, nine years after joining the Line, he was selected as an assistant manager with special responsibility for crew appointments. It was Huskisson who appointed the crew for *Southern Cross*, and it was Huskisson who was "management co-ordinator" for *Northern Star* from the time her keel plate was laid in the Walker-on-Tyne yard. He had to "know everything" about the new ship and the progress of her building, fitting out, and crew appointments and to keep Lord Sanderson fully informed. Once the *Star*'s maiden voyage began his responsibilities changed to the supervision of dock labour. He was appointed chairman of the London Shipowners Dock Labour Committee, and a vice-chairman of the Shipping Federation.

In some ways the problems of management facing MacConochie and Russell and the Line's directors at the end of 1963 differed from those which confronted Lord Sanderson and Keville immediately after the War; in others they remained much the same.

The urgency had passed for rebuilding and renovating the fleet. This had been steadily and skilfully accomplished, so that by the end of 1964 the Line's twenty-ninth ship to be built since the War was launched at the Vickers-Armstrong yards at Walker-on-Tyne—the refrigerated cargo-liner *Laurentic*. Orders were also placed for two more cargo-liners.

On the other hand, during the last few years of Lord Sanderson's chairmanship, increasing competition developed from foreign lines for passengers and cargo, and this continued. Problems of the slow turn-round in port of cargo-ships and congestion also remained, and their solution was being approached by the formation of streamlining committees in London and New Zealand and similar moves in the Australian trade.

Some of these problems are no part of the story of *Southern Cross* and *Northern Star*. This, indeed, reflects one of the most marked changes in travel between Britain, New Zealand, Australia, and South Africa since the War: the great number of young people travelling to and fro on "working holidays".

During the inter-War years, particularly the late nineteen-thirties, most ships sailed with half their passenger berths empty. Even low fares could not offset the by-products of the phase of unemployment.

Whatever their other preoccupations, unemployment has not shadowed the lives of the post-War generation.

There has been a steady flow of young men and women seeing the outside world for the first time, and influencing Shaw Savill to compete with other lines, to study routes, and to include as many interesting ports of call as possible. First Suva, Tahiti, Panama, Curaçao, and Trinidad were added, then Rarotonga, Acapulco, Barbados, Miami, and Bermuda. Soon Mauritius may be on the route of *Southern Cross* and *Northern Star*, and other ports being contemplated include Laurenço Marques, Luanda, and Dakar. The holiday aspect of the working holiday will soon have even more attractions.

Improvements are made continually in both ships. For instance, a Seahorse Room has been added to *Southern Cross*. By day an area near the bathing pools is used as a sun-bathing lido. This is transformed each evening into a room by electrically operated roller shutters and covered by a coloured canopy. Sun-bathers now become dancers, the bar opens again. The *Cross* now has a launderette with a number of automatic washing machines; more carpets have been laid in *Northern Star*—in the forward lounge and the smoke-room.

In due time the Shaw Savill Line will concentrate on a successor to *Southern Cross* and *Northern Star*. Already new ideas are being examined, new machinery inspected, developments compiled. Some, indeed, are in use—for instance, a computer in the engine-room. It works through a voyage recording oil pressures, temperatures, and speeds; it logs all this information for the perusal of the chief engineer and also for the records of the superintendent engineer in Leadenhall Street. And just as forklift trucks are now normal equipment for loading and discharging cargo on the quayside, so they are being used aboard ships whose tank-tops and decks have been specially strengthened. Other developments are known by the unattractive words "palletization" and "containerization"; they too will influence the design of new ships.

Designs, developments, power, cost, the flow of passengers, and the preponderance of any particular age group among passengers—all these and other facets will be reviewed, revised, and deliberated until the last moment before a new tender is placed.

"Shaw Savill have been pioneers from their earliest days, and we shall continue to pioneer within reasonable limits," says John MacConochie whenever he discusses the future.

"We face increasing competition, but this is inevitable with the continuing flow of settlers to Australia and New Zealand from Continental countries as well as Britain. The populations of these southern Dominions are growing, particularly in Australia, and several shipping companies are tending to gravitate their passenger-ships to that part of the world.

"You may be certain that the Shaw Savill flag will continue to fly on the oceans and around these coasts just as it has for the last hundred years and more. The pattern of trade is tending to change, but we believe that Britain will continue as the main market for the southern Dominions during the foreseeable future, and that both Australia and New Zealand will remain important British customers.

"And people will still want to travel in comfort and at leisure at reasonable cost. In many ways the world is a smaller place today than when the sailing-ships were trading the seas. But the distances are just the same and the oceans are no smaller, and they still have to be crossed. The sea will always provide us with a future. We live near the sea. We live by the sea. Let us never forget it."

Index